Diale

Dialectical Behaviour Therapy (DBT) is a psychotherapeutic approach designed particularly to treat the problems of chronically suicidal individuals with borderline personality disorder (BPD). The therapy articulates a series of principles that effectively guide clinicians in responding to suicidal and other behaviours that challenge them when treating this population.

Dialectical Behaviour Therapy highlights 30 distinctive features of the treatment and uses extensive clinical examples to demonstrate how the theory translates into practice. In *Part 1: The Distinctive Theoretical Features of DBT*, the authors introduce us to the three foundations on which the treatment rests – behaviourism, Zen and dialectics – and how these integrate. In *Part 2: The Distinctive Practical Features of DBT*, Swales and Heard describe how the therapy applies these principles to the treatment of clients with borderline personality disorder and elucidate the distinctive conceptual twists in the application of cognitive and behavioural procedures within the treatment.

This book provides a clear and structured overview of a complex treatment. It is written for both practising clinicians and students wishing to learn more about DBT and how it differs from the other cognitive-behaviour therapies.

Michaela A. Swales is a lecturer–practitioner in clinical psychology at Bangor University and a consultant clinical psychologist at the North Wales Adolescent Service, North Wales NHS Trust. She is the Director of the British Isles DBT Training Team.

Heidi L. Heard is a senior trainer for BehavioralTech, USA and an international consultant and supervisor in Dialectical Behaviour Therapy. She has written extensively about DBT and borderline personality disorder.

Cognitive-behavioural therapy (CBT) occupies a central position in the move towards evidence-based practice and is frequently used in the clinical environment. Yet there is no one universal approach to CBT and clinicians speak of first-, second-, and even third-wave approaches.

This series provides straightforward, accessible guides to a number of CBT methods, clarifying the distinctive features of each approach. The series editor, Windy Dryden, successfully brings together experts from each discipline to summarize the 30 main aspects of their approach divided into theoretical and practical features.

The CBT Distinctive Features Series will be essential reading for psychotherapists, counsellors, and psychologists of all orientations who want to learn more about the range of new and developing cognitive-behavioural approaches.

Titles in the series:

For further information about this series please visit:
www.routledgementalhealth.com/cbt-distinctive-features

Dialectical Behaviour Therapy

Distinctive Features

Michaela A. Swales and Heidi L. Heard

Routledge
Taylor & Francis Group

LONDON AND NEW YORK

First published 2009 by Routledge
27 Church Road, Hove, East Sussex BN3 2FA

Simultaneously published in the USA and Canada
by Routledge
270 Madison Avenue, New York NY 10016

Reprinted 2009 and 2010 (twice)

Routledge is an imprint of the Taylor & Francis Group, an Informa
business

Typeset in Times by Garfield Morgan,
Swansea, West Glamorgan
Printed and bound in Great Britain by
TJ International Ltd, Padstow, Cornwall
Cover design by Sandra Heath

British Library Cataloguing in Publication Data
A catalogue record for this book is available from the British Library

Library of Congress Cataloging-in-Publication Data
Swales, Michaela A., 1965–
   Dialectical behaviour therapy : distinctive features / Michaela A.
Swales and Heidi L. Heard.
      p. ; cm.
   Includes bibliographical references and index.
   ISBN 978-0-415-44457-6 (hbk) – ISBN 978-0-415-44458-3 (pbk.) 1.
Borderline personality disorder–Treatment. 2. Dialectical behavior
therapy. I. Heard, Heidi L. II. Title.
   [DNLM: 1. Borderline Personality Disorder–therapy. 2.
CognitiveTherapy–methods. 3. Suicide–prevention & control. WM
190 S972d 2009]
   RC569.5.B67S93 2009
   616.85'852–dc22

                                                      2008023712

ISBN: 978-0-415-44457-6 (hbk)
ISBN: 978-0-415-44458-3 (pbk)

To our parents
Pat and Eric Brookes, Tom Swales, Margaret
and Jerry Heard

Contents

Introduction

Dialectical Behaviour Therapy (DBT) is a psychotherapeutic approach designed to treat the problems of chronically suicidal individuals with borderline personality disorder (BPD). This book articulates the principles of the treatment, focusing particularly on principles that distinguish DBT from other cognitive-behavioural treatments. In common with all the books in this series, this volume has two parts, the first devoted to theory and the second to practice. The theoretical component of the book illustrates distinctive features of DBT relating to its three foundations: behaviourism (Points 6–8), dialectical philosophy (Point 3) and Zen (Point 9). The second part of the book focuses on practice and how the philosophical and theoretical underpinnings of the treatment flow into the treatment structure and strategies.

DBT is based on a transactional bio-social theory of the aetiology of the affect regulation problems of BPD (Point 4). Individuals with a biological emotional vulnerability and raised in environments that systematically invalidate their inner experiences and overt behaviours develop deficits in both the capacity and the motivation to manage their emotions and other aspects of their lives (Point 5). DBT treatment programmes comprehensively address these capability and motivational deficits, providing a multi-modal, staged treatment that targets the full range of comorbid disorders of the client in a hierarchical manner (Points 11–17). DBT integrates strategies from cognitive-behavioural treatment (Points 19–24) with aspects of Zen practice (Points 9 and 21). The treatment utilizes the dialectical philosophy (Points 3 and 25) to synthesize these two contrasting perspectives into a coherent set of treatment principles.

Terminology and use of clinical examples

We are aware of the debate in relation to terminology denoting the individual seeking assistance from the therapy and the therapist. We can see the validity in the use of most of the frequently used terms (e.g. client, patient, service user), but, we have selected the most commonly used term of client for this book. The individual component of DBT is a psychotherapy, as defined by Corsini and Wedding (1989). It would, therefore, be appropriate to denote the person delivering this component of the treatment as the individual psychotherapist. In some jurisdictions, however, the term psychotherapist indicates a separate professional discipline with a distinct training route or indicates the use of a particular theoretical model. We therefore use the term "individual therapist" to avoid confusion.

In terms of clinical examples, we have drawn both on our direct experience of clinical work and also our extensive experience of training and supervising therapists working with individuals diagnosed with BPD. As is customary, we have created "composite" case scenarios and have deliberately used examples that reflect common responses or typical sequences of events that we have encountered over the years. Thus, no example is of an actual client or therapist. Any resemblance to an actual person is accidental.

In summary, this book highlights theoretical and practice principles that distinguish DBT. The book does not, therefore, describe all the principles of the treatment and consequently can not substitute for reading the treatment manuals (Linehan, 1993a, 1993b). Neither is this book a substitute for training and supervision in the treatment. We highlight characteristics of DBT to assist practitioners in deciding whether this treatment approach interests them sufficiently to read or train further and to provide a précis of the treatment, with clinical examples, for practitioners who have already received training. Clients may also find this book useful in orienting them to the main features of the treatment and helping them to decide whether they wish to pursue treatment.

Acknowledgements

We both owe a tremendous debt to the developer of DBT, Marsha M. Linehan. She has developed a treatment that demands an extensive and thorough understanding of different theories and philosophies and that translates these foundations into life-saving and life-changing interventions. Marsha has inspired, challenged and taught us.

She has motivated us to deliver and train others in DBT with the compassionate rigour that she brings to treatment development and evaluation. We only hope that in this volume we have done justice to the richness, compassion and accuracy of her work.

We would like to express our gratitude to Messrs Strunck & White for their invaluable editorial assistance and witty contributions to developing our writing.

Michaela Swales and Heidi Heard
December 2007

Professionally I am indebted to many mentors and colleagues who over the years have supported me. Mark Williams, my PhD supervisor, and more latterly colleague and friend, first introduced me to DBT. As a novice clinical psychologist struggling to help self-harming adolescent clients, I was delighted when Mark, with his customary vision and generosity, funded my Intensive Training in DBT in Seattle. I met Heidi at this training and the journey to writing this book began. I am also indebted to many colleagues in my clinical practice at the North Wales Adolescent Service who, over the years, have given me the freedom to learn and develop DBT and have frequently managed the DBT programme during my absences for training and academic duties. I am particularly grateful for the graciousness with which they allowed me to take a break from clinical work to write this book (among other things) at a challenging time for the service. Similarly, senior managers within my employing organization, North Wales NHS Trust, supported my academic work in DBT at a time of increased clinical pressure and financial constraint. I am grateful for their willingness. I would also like to thank my clients who have been my best teachers. Their courage and tenacity motivates me as a clinician and as a trainer and supervisor in DBT. Thanks are due to my assistant Barbara Baragwanath who is always flexible and willing. Without her input the whole process of finishing this book would have been all the more painful.

Personally my greatest debt, as always, is to my family. My husband, Richard, and children, Thomas and Caitlin, have contributed in many practical and emotional ways to the writing of this book. All three have tolerated my absences, both physical and mental, with good grace. My greatest thanks go to them.

Michaela Swales
Llandudno, UK, December 2007

I would like to thank colleagues who have supported my work in DBT and taught me the requisite skills for that work. DBT co-trainers and supervisees have particularly provided the inspiration for this book, and therefore I want to highlight my special appreciation for them. I am also grateful to clients who have accepted my fallibility and helped me to become a better clinician. Finally, I would like to thank my family and friends for their enduring support throughout the process of writing this book. I especially want to express my gratitude to my friend and fellow author, Deborah Gross, for her validation and problem solving during our many conversations about the book.

Heidi Heard
St Louis, USA, December 2007

Part 1

THE DISTINCTIVE THEORETICAL FEATURES OF DBT

1

Principle-driven treatment

Your office phone rings shortly after 5.30 p.m. on a Friday evening. You've had a long and stressful week and are anticipating a relaxing weekend. One of your clients is on the line. She reveals that she is in a suicidal crisis and is currently standing by a major transport bridge in your area (she is vague about which one) with the intention of jumping off. Her plan had been to leave a message for you on the office answer phone apologizing for her action. She has flattened affect and indicates that several events have occurred in the last 48 hours that indicate to you that her already chronic risk has increased. She has frequently been hospitalized in similar situations in the past, but this has rarely helped. She expresses extreme hopelessness and remains reluctant to talk. Do you remain on the phone and try to soothe her out of the plan by offering extra support or other interventions? Do you remain matter of fact, attempt to solve the problem or problems that led to the crisis? Do you try to find out where she is and then send emergency services to her aid? And if you do, do you stay on the phone while you wait for them to arrive? Do you try to arrange hospitalization? What do you do and, perhaps more importantly, what principles do you use to decide what to do?

Dialectical Behaviour Therapy (DBT) articulates a series of principles to help the practitioner decide what to do in circumstances like these. The treatment also describes how to integrate responses during crises with an overarching treatment plan. These principles are designed to enhance therapist effectiveness in applying the treatment adherently while remaining maximally responsive to the client.

DBT flexibly applies the treatment principles within a highly structured and comprehensive treatment programme as applying traditional cognitive-behavioural treatment to clients with a diagnosis of bordeline personality disorder (BPD) presents several challenges (Linehan, 1993a). Frequently, clients present varied problems from week to week, each of which may require a different CBT treatment protocol. For example, one week the client may report extensive panic attacks and avoidance of social activities; the following week, the presented problems are bingeing and vomiting; the week after the client presents in an acute suicidal crisis. The extent of comorbidity within the client group makes adhering to the procedure of any single traditional cognitive-behavioural treatment problematic and may account, in part, for the impaired effectiveness of such treatments for clients with a personality disorder diagnosis (Shea et al., 1990; Steiger & Stotland, 1996). Following a highly structured treatment protocol, with a clear and consistent therapeutic focus and a unified formulation, in the face of multiple and varied problems is almost impossible. Furthermore, clients diagnosed with BPD frequently present with therapy-interfering behaviours (e.g. not attending sessions, complaints, hostility toward the therapy, therapist, or both) that add to the challenge of delivering therapy. Under these circumstances, many therapists report a "war of attrition" occurring between the client and the therapist. The therapist persistently attempts and fails to implement the protocol, and the client deems the therapist's efforts more and more irrelevant. Eventually, the therapist delivers the antithesis of a structured, focused intervention and instead follows the client impulsively, adding whatever strategy he or she thinks may prove helpful as a problem whizzes by. DBT endeavours to steer a dialectical course between these two extremes.

To counteract these challenges in delivering a traditional cognitive-behavioural treatment for clients with BPD, Linehan developed a treatment that is more principle than protocol-driven. At the time Linehan developed DBT, cognitive-behavioural treatments were already demonstrating their considerable effectiveness in treating a range of Axis I disorders. Derived from basic research and associated cognitive-behavioural models, disorder-based treatments derive a clear series of treatment tasks or steps to modify the processes underlying each respective disorder. Each treatment task or step may have specific strategies associated with it. For example, in cognitive therapy for panic disorder the therapist demonstrates to the client that hyperventilation, driven by catastrophic inter-pretations of normal bodily sensations, leads to physiological sensations that the client further misinterprets. The therapist then proceeds to intervene in this vicious cycle using a range of cognitive and behavioural techniques. Because of the high level of structure these treatments provide in terms of conceptualiza-tion and the clarity with which they specify each step of imple-mentation, traditional cognitive-behavioural treatments can be described as protocol-driven treatments.[1]

Although all treatments are principle based, not all are principle driven. Principle-driven treatments use a guiding theory to assist the therapist in drawing and following a map of the direction of travel within therapy. All treatments have a theory of the aetiology and maintenance of the psychiatric disorder that guides the therapist in deciding which strategies to employ to ameliorate clients' difficulties. Often the high level of specification of treatment strategies in CBT, however, can lead

---

1 Notwithstanding these characteristics, the effective implementation of these treatments still requires the development of an individualized formulation, the capacity to develop and to maintain a collaborative working alliance with the client and a degree of flexibility in the application of the strategies. As a consequence of the high degree of specification, CBT approaches are often viewed as merely a series of techniques that can be applied in the absence of a theoretical and conceptual understanding. Application of techniques in the absence of wider understanding is unlikely to be effective (Tarrier & Wykes, 2004). Delivery of these well-specified CBT treatments still requires extensive training and supervision.

the therapist to moving away from principles and to following a series of procedures instead. The therapist may only return to principles at times of difficulty or challenge within the therapy. In a protocol-driven treatment, detailed maps of the therapy journey are available with all roadways marked and the defining features of the landscape defined. Therapists have a clear idea of how they will reach the destination, although several possible routes may be available. In a principle-driven treatment therapists must constantly attend to the key principles. Therapists have minimally detailed maps, with few landmarks and only parts of roads and some features marked. In the absence of existing roads to the destination, the therapist first surveys the landscape to determine the best strategy for building roads to the destination. A protocol-driven therapist needs to drive well, especially over rough terrain in poor weather conditions. A principle-driven therapist must also drive well, but also must know something about surveying the territory, building roads and, of course, drawing maps to minimize the chance of becoming lost.

In comparison to protocol-driven treatments, delivering principle-driven treatments presents at least three additional challenges. First, the therapist must assess and determine which principles to apply and how to apply them in any given circumstance. Many therapists prefer simply to develop and apply a rule and in learning the treatment constantly seek to distil the principles into a set or rules.

Second, in principle-driven treatments usually multiple principles are relevant at any one time. For example, DBT provides clients with feedback about the impact of their behaviour on the therapist (self-involving self-disclosure). Therapists should not follow this principle ubiquitously, however. In some circumstances, providing this feedback may contradict another key principle of the treatment, namely minimizing the reinforcement of problematic behaviours. For example, in response to the therapist's confrontation about non-attendance at skills group, a client verbally threatened the therapist who then experienced anxiety and avoided further confrontation. Sharing this sequence of events with the client may motivate the client to change, but only if the client does not intend to frighten the therapist. If the client wishes to frighten the therapist in order to stop the confrontation, the therapist self-disclosure is unlikely to motivate the client to stop the threats. In these circumstances, the therapist may need to manage his or her own anxiety while maintaining a confrontational stance towards the client about solving non-attendance at group. Alternatively, to counteract the reinforcing contingencies the therapist may highlight other aversive contingencies for the client. For example, how the client's behaviour blocks another of the client's treatment goals such as building and maintaining supportive relationships.

The final difficulty for therapists with principle-based treatments relates to the relative familiarity of some principles compared to others. Because DBT integrates principles from a range of therapeutic and non-therapeutic traditions, therapists from all orientations find familiar principles within the treatment. The challenge for any therapist learning DBT is to attend to learning and applying novel principles rather than only relying on familiar beliefs and practices.

2

Integrative treatment

Perhaps few therapies emphasize integration so explicitly on as many disparate levels as DBT. The treatment is integrative in the "dialectical/developmental" sense of the word (Stricker & Gold, 1993), meaning that it emphasizes the "open-ended dialogical process in which differences are examined and novel integrations are welcomed" (p. 7). Thus, while at any given moment DBT constitutes a single, unified psychotherapy, it also changes continuously as new developments become incorporated rather than avoided, rather like a client effectively participating in therapy.

As the treatment's name suggests, the concepts of synthesis and integration permeate DBT in several ways. First, reflecting the broad academic setting in which the treatment evolved, Linehan (1993a) proposed a transactional theory of the aetiology and maintenance of BPD that integrates both biological and environmental models, as well as developmental and learning perspectives. The treatment continues to adapt in response to new data from these areas.

Second, the treatment evolved out of a tension between an emphasis on change as the essence of CBTs versus an emphasis on radical acceptance of the client in the moment as a requisite context for treating clients with BPD. Initially, Linehan applied standard behaviour therapy procedures to chronically parasuicidal clients. Compared with most clients who successfully complete behavioural programmes, these clients had significantly more behaviours to target, poorer treatment compliance, and higher treatment drop-out. The difficulties of forming a collaborative relationship, maintaining safety, keeping a stable set of goals and priorities across sessions and unrelenting crises made the application of traditional CBT in any straightforward, manualized way fraught with difficulty.

The difficulty in applying standard CBTs suggested an inherent poorness of fit between these therapies and clients with BPD. Linehan hypothesized that the therapy-interfering behaviours occurred as a result of the treatment's perceived focus on changing behaviours, ranging from emotions and cognitions to overt behaviour. She suggested that the clients experienced the treatment not only as invalidating of specific behaviours but as invalidating of themselves as a whole. Being told that one must change is inherently invalidating to oneself, even if one agrees with the statement. In a sense, therapists validated clients' fears that they indeed could not trust their own reactions, cognitive interpretations, or behavioural responses. Research by Swann and colleagues (Swann, Stein-Seroussi, & Giesler, 1992) may explain how such perceived invalidation leads to problematic behaviour in therapy. Their research revealed that when an individual's basic self-constructs are not verified, the individual's arousal increases. The increased arousal then leads to cognitive dysregulation and the failure to process new information. The bio-social theory described later would suggest that BPD clients are particularly sensitive to any potentially invalidating cues and more likely to become highly aroused.

To balance the emphasis on change, Linehan began to integrate the principles of Zen (e.g. Aitken, 1982) and the associated practice of mindfulness (e.g. Hanh, 1987), which describe acceptance at its most radical level. Zen encourages radical acceptance of the moment without change. We will discuss Zen and mindfulness in greater detail later. Unfortunately, as Linehan further proposed, a therapeutic approach based on unconditional acceptance and validation of the client's behaviours may prove equally problematic and, paradoxically, invalidating. If the therapist only urges the client to accept and self-validate, it can appear that the therapist does not take the client's problems seriously. Without attention to change and solving problems, the client's personal experience of life as intolerable and unendurable is invalidated, and therapy-interfering behaviours will likely occur.

The tensions arising from Linehan's attempt to integrate the principles of behaviourism with those of Zen required a framework that could house opposing views. The dialectical philosophy, which highlights the process of synthesizing oppositions, provides such a framework. Through the continual resolution of tensions between theory and research versus clinical experience and between Western psychology versus Eastern philosophy, DBT evolved in a manner similar to the theoretical integration model described by psychotherapy integration researchers (Arkowitz, 1989, 1992; Norcross & Newman, 1992).

Third, in response to the complexity and severity of problems presented by borderline clients, the structural aspects of DBT are integrated to support each other. This appears most obviously in the relationships among the standard treatment modalities (individual therapy, skills training, phone consultation and team consultation), which we describe in greater detail later. Each modality supports the work of another. For example, group skills trainers help the clients to acquire the basic elements of each skills set and to strengthen those skills. Then, the individual therapist further strengthens the skills, and telephone coaching facilitates generalizing the skills to everyday life. If the individual therapist had to teach the basic elements as well, substantially less time would remain for implementing other solutions. Similarly, without the support of individual therapy and telephone coaching, many clients would either not use the skills or would use them ineffectively. Of note, a study (Linehan, Heard, & Armstrong, 1995) comparing one year of standard community psychotherapy (SCP) to SCP plus a concurrent DBT skills training group found that addition of the skills training group did not produce better treatment outcomes than SCP alone. Though future research may demonstrate that DBT skills training has no impact on outcomes, it may also prove that its impact depends upon its integration with the other treatment modalities.

In contrast with a common practice in treatment as usual to "bolt on" additional interventions, DBT requires the primary therapist to identify the specific function(s) of any additional intervention and to clarify how it will interact with the DBT programme. Clinical experience would suggest that without such clarification additional interventions interact less efficiently at best. They may also negate DBT interventions and increase the likelihood of therapy-interfering behaviour by the client or "splitting" among staff. For example, adding a "support worker" in response to a client's increased suicidal communications may increase those communications in the future if the client values having as much contact with healthcare providers as possible. To minimize the likelihood of such problems, the treatment requires that the client does not participate concurrently in any other intensive psychotherapy.

Lastly, DBT integrates strategies and techniques from across the field of psychology and beyond. Though primarily a CBT, DBT also employs techniques from other clinical interventions, such as crisis management, and from other areas of psychology. For example, it requires clients to agree upon goals and make an explicit commitment to the treatment because of the social psychology research (e.g. Hall, Havassy, & Wasserman, 1990; Wang & Katzev, 1990) that indicates that individuals will more likely follow through with a plan or remain in a situation if they have committed to that plan or situation. To facilitate this process, Linehan (1993a) adapted two social psychology commitment techniques: the foot-in-the-door (Freedman & Fraser, 1966) and the door-in-the-face (Cialdini et al., 1975). Finally, reaching beyond Western psychology, the treatment interweaves the Zen practice of mindfulness. DBT modifies the technical eclecticism approach of psychotherapy integration (Arkowitz, 1992; Norcross & Newman, 1992) by requiring that all techniques fit within a dialectical framework synthesizing behaviourism and key principles from Zen. The reliance on a coherent set of principles may prove crucial to treating the therapist, as well as the client. When treating difficult populations, therapists desperately require a coherent framework on which they can depend.

3

Dialectical principles

As the underlying philosophy of DBT, dialectics describes the process by which the development of the therapy and progress within the therapy occurs and by which conflicts that impede development or progress are resolved. Ancient Greek philosophers first developed dialectics as a method to improve logic, but modern writers, starting with Hegel, have extended it into a philosophy to explain the evolution of many aspects of life, including economics (see Tucker, 1978, for Karl Marx) and science (Kuhn, 1970). Dialectics has been defined as: ". . . the concept of the contradiction of opposites (thesis and antithesis) and their continual resolution (synthesis)" (*Webster's New World Dictionary*, 1964, p. 404). Linehan's application of dialectics (1993a; Linehan & Schmidt, 1995) was influenced by work in the areas of evolutionary biology (Levins & Lewontin, 1985), cognitive development (Basseches, 1984) and the development of self (Kegan, 1982). DBT particularly emphasizes three dialectical assumptions regarding the nature of reality, namely that reality is: (1) interrelated or systemic; (2) oppositional or heterogeneous; and (3) continuously changing.

Interrelatedness

Dialectics stresses the interrelatedness and unity of reality. The dialectical philosophy emphasizes relationships within and between systems and the complexity of causal connections. Levins and Lewontin (1985) described this aspect of dialectics: "Parts and wholes evolve in consequence of their relationship, and the relationship itself evolves. These are the properties of things that we call dialectical: that one thing cannot exist

15

without the other, that one acquires its properties from its relations to the other" (p. 3).

To analyse the factors that maintain problematic behaviour, the therapist considers two basic levels at which the client may experience dysfunction within the systems that influence their behaviour. The first level includes overlapping and mutually influential systems within the individual such as bio-chemical systems, affective regulation systems and information-processing systems. For example, dysregulated serotonin may lead to affective instability. Affective dysregulation often interferes with cognition. If the cognitive dysregulation includes a disruption of problem-solving abilities, this disruption could lead to a crisis that, in turn, further increases affective dysregu-lation. While multiple dysregulations may require multiple treatment interventions, a systemic approach also foresees how any single treatment interventions may influence multiple systems. For example, effective pharmacotherapy may regulate serotonin intake such that the chain described above never begins. Alternatively, enhancing emotion-regulation skills may help the client to cope effectively with biological changes and thus minimize the potential for impaired information proces-sing and problems.

The second level of systemic dysregulation involves the many interpersonal systems, such as family and culture, and other environmental systems that influence behaviour. To obtain an accurate understanding of the client's behaviour, the therapist must assess these influences as well as biological and psycho-logical factors. Many clients live in or interact with systems that reinforce problematic behaviour or punish skilful behaviour. For example, the hospitalization of a client for suicidal beha-viour may actually reinforce the behaviour if the hospitalization provides desirable consequences such as more warmth and caring from staff than the client receives elsewhere or fewer onerous responsibilities (e.g. coping with children, finding housing) that the client cannot otherwise avoid. Alternatively, a client's attempts to search for employment may be punished by a family in which everyone else lives on unemployment benefits and criticizes the client for "acting above" his or her family.

Within the process of therapy, the DBT therapist attends to the system of the therapeutic relationship and to the tensions or therapy-interfering behaviours that can arise. Dialectics specifically directs the therapist's attention toward transactions that occur between the therapist and client and accepts that the therapist is part of and, therefore, influenced by the therapeutic context. The DBT therapist views therapy as a system in which the therapist and client reciprocally influence each other. For example, if a client became verbally aggressive every time the therapist tried to address a presenting problem, the therapist may become less likely to target that problem. In this scenario the client would have punished the therapist's therapeutic behaviour, and the therapist may have reinforced the client's aggressive behaviour. Altering transactional developments such as this can prove rather difficult when one is part of the system. DBT therapists, however, participate in another treatment system, the consultation team, which functions to counteract such developments in the therapy by providing the motivation for the therapist to return to the therapeutic behaviour.

Opposition

Dialectics also focuses attention on the complexity of the whole. Reality is not static but consists of opposing forces in tension, the thesis and anti-thesis. Development occurs as these oppositions proceed toward synthesis and as a new set of opposing forces emerges from the synthesis. The philosophy suggests a heterogeneous world in which reality is neither black nor white nor grey.

In therapy, tensions can arise within the client, within the therapist, between the client and therapist or between the therapist and the larger treatment system. Examples of tensions that occur between the therapist and the client include: (a) the client's belief that taking drugs is the solution and the therapist's belief that taking drugs is the problem; (b) the client's belief that only hospitalization will prevent suicide now and the therapist's belief that hospitalization may increase the probability of a future suicide; and (c) the client's wish for more contact with the therapist and the therapist's wish to observe his or her own limits. To resolve conflicts the therapy searches for syntheses. The most effective syntheses are generally those that validate some aspect of both sides of the debate and move toward more effective behaviour. For example, in the first scenario above, if the client considers drugs as a solution because they decrease overwhelming anxiety, the therapy may achieve a synthesis by identifying anxiety reduction as a valid therapy goal. With this as the accepted goal, drug abuse would no longer be a valid solution, as it will tend, directly and indirectly, to increase, not decrease, anxiety in the long term. The therapy would instead focus on the client developing more skilful means to prevent and to manage anxiety.

Linehan (1993a) suggested that the central opposition in psychotherapy occurs between change and acceptance. The relationship between change and acceptance forms the basic paradox and context of treatment. Therapeutic change can occur only in the context of acceptance of what is, and the act of acceptance itself is change. Linehan (1993c) defined acceptance as "the fully open experience of what is without distortion, adding judgement of good/bad, clinging or pushing away" and as "the radical truth without the haze of what we want it to be or what we don't want it to be". Linehan (1993c) defined "radical acceptance" as "an act of the total person that is allowing of this one moment, this reality, without discrimination". Thus, acceptance of a destructive act requires not only acceptance that the act has occurred, but also that it caused damage and that it may need repair to ameliorate that damage.

Moving rapidly, the DBT therapist balances acceptance strategies, which accept the client in the moment, and change strategies, which attempt to alter the client's behaviour. The therapy strives to help the client understand that responses may both prove valid and present a problem to solve. For example, a client who fears not having sufficient skills to cope when the therapist leaves town for a holiday is a valid response from a client who has few coping skills and functions better when the therapist remains in town. On the other hand, the client must learn new skills to cope with the separation because the therapist will leave town. One synthesis that may validate both positions and lead to treatment progress may be to schedule an extra session prior to the holiday to focus exclusively on acquiring skills to cope with the therapist's absence.

The ability of the DBT therapist to synthesize acceptance and change is enhanced through synthesizing aspects of Zen with behaviourism. While CBTs provide the technology of change, Zen practice provides the technology of acceptance. Furthermore, Linehan and Schmidt (1995) have suggested that the differences between Zen and behaviourism parallel the debate within dialectics between "dialectical idealism" and "dialectical materialism" (Reese, 1993). The authors state:

> Although the philosophy of dialectical materialism relevant to DBT (corresponding to behavior theory as a foundation of DBT) views humans as imposing an order on an uncaring world, dialectical idealism (corresponding to the roots of DBT in Zen psychology) believes that people can recognize and experience a unity and pattern inherent in the organization of the universe.
>
> (Linehan & Schmidt, 1995, p. 558)

By synthesizing Zen and behaviourism, the treatment can help suicidal clients "to come to grips with a life that both is inherently meaningful and entirely irrelevant" (Linehan & Schmidt, 1995, p. 556). Of course, the categorization of behaviour therapy and Zen practice into change and acceptance is only relative, as each practice contains elements of both acceptance and change. Like most therapies, CBT requires therapists to treat clients as they currently are, not as the therapist would like them to be, and Zen emphasizes the importance of impermanence.

Change

Dialectics highlights change as a fundamental aspect of reality. Change is the very essence of experience, and both the individual and the environment undergo continuous transition by a process of opposition resolving through synthesis. The change or development, however, may not occur along a positive trajectory.

To some degree, all therapies foster change, but they differ in what type of change they promote and to what degree. Because of its assumption that clients' lives are currently unbearable to them, DBT clearly focuses on change. In addition to influencing change in the client's behaviour, the treatment allows the therapist extensive freedom to change as well. For example, as the therapy relationship develops, the therapist may become willing to expand various limits (e.g. willingness to accept phone calls, using examples of self as a coping model) as one would expand limits in a non-therapy relationship over time. The therapist's limits may also contract as a result of changes in the therapy relationship (e.g. client begins to phone the therapist too often or shares the therapist's self-disclosure with other clients) or the therapist's life (e.g. therapist has a baby or is moving house). Allowing natural change creates a therapeutic context that more closely matches the world outside of therapy and may help the client to generalize learning to non-therapy relationships. The therapist does not try to protect the client from natural change but instead tries to help the client learn to cope with such change. For example, when group skills trainers rotate in to and out of an ongoing group, the trainers may directly target the clients' distress by helping them to practise some of the relevant skills that they have learned during skills training. DBT only requires therapists to remain constant in adhering to the principles of the treatment.

Both behaviourism and Zen discuss change but in slightly different ways. Behaviour therapy promotes change by using interventions such as contingency management, exposure, problem solving or skills training that require the client and therapist to actively change the client's emotions, thoughts, overt behaviour or environment. In contrast, in Zen practice neither the student nor the master intentionally tries to change the student, but instead they mindfully accept reality as it occurs. Behaviour therapy and Zen practice thus offer two approaches to change in therapy. For example, though behavioural procedures can reduce suicidal behaviour by teaching the client how to actively reduce suicidal urges, Zen practice can reduce suicidal behaviour by teaching the client how to allow and observe the urges without acting on them. These two approaches to suicidal behaviour reciprocally enhance each other. On the one hand, an important step in reducing suicidal urges is to increase awareness of those variables that control the urges. On the other hand, if one observes the urges without reinforcing them through action, the urges will naturally decrease over time.

4

Emphasis on the primacy of affect

In comparison to many cognitive-behavioural treatments, and particularly cognitive therapies, DBT especially emphasizes the role of affect as a key causal variable. Unlike some forms of cognitive-behavioural treatment, DBT does not necessarily require cognition as a mediating variable between prompting events and affect. DBT conceptualizes affect as the totality of the internal system response following a prompting event. Linehan (1993a) hypothesized that a heightened vulnerability to these systemic responses and the inability to regulate such responses leads to many of the behaviours associated with BPD.

Emotion as a total system response

DBT emphasizes the totality of the multi-system response to affective cues. In this conceptualization, emotions comprise internal biological responses (e.g. changes in neurotransmitters, changes in blood flow and muscle tension), internal sensations (e.g. "butterflies" in the stomach, experience of the face flushing, sensation of experiencing the emotion—in other models this sense experience is often referred to as the "emotion"—and action urges associated with the emotion), external changes in behaviour (e.g. facial movement, verbal behaviour and overt actions) and cognitions. Linehan highlights that this multi-system response may be more of an automatic response to the prompting event in some circumstances (e.g. flight/fight responses, classically conditioned responses) and may be mediated by online cognitive processing (e.g. judgements, interpretations) in others. At different times, DBT therapists attend to all aspects of the emotional response and to modifying affect, regardless of the level of automaticity of the response. DBT identifies two particular problems with the affective system for clients with BPD: emotional vulnerability and an inability to modulate affect.

Emotional vulnerability

Linehan (1993a) hypothesized that clients who meet criteria for BPD have a biological predisposition to emotional dysregulation. This emotional vulnerability may result from a genetic predisposition, the biological response to intrauterine adverse events or early trauma. Though current data support a biological basis for emotional vulnerability (Bateman & Fonagy, 2004; Linehan, 1993a) the primacy of emotional vulnerability in BPD remains a hypothesis that warrants further investigation.

The emotional vulnerability described by Linehan consists of three characteristics:

- *Sensitivity to emotional stimuli.* The client has a heightened awareness towards emotional stimuli and reacts to lower levels of stimulus than would the average person.
- *Reactivity to emotional stimulus.* The client responds rapidly and with a high degree of intensity to emotional stimuli.
- *Slow return to baseline.* Emotional arousal decays more slowly than in the average person contributing to subsequent emotional sensitivity.

In the context of intense levels of affect that decline only slowly, other systems become dysregulated resulting in the behaviours of the BPD diagnosis. For example, extreme emotional arousal may disinhibit overt behaviour (impulsive and parasuicidal behaviours), disrupt interpersonal relationships (chaotic relationships, frantic efforts to avoid abandonment), dysregulate thinking (paranoid and dissociative responses) and destabilize the sense of self (sense of emptiness, identity disturbance). Thus, DBT conceptualizes the behaviours of the BPD diagnosis as either natural consequences of experiencing intense emotional dysregulation or learned attempts to reduce these extremes. Naturally, disturbance in any of the other behavioural systems often further dysregulates affect and compounds the client's difficulties. Intervention to ameliorate the difficulty in any one system, however, has the potential to positively benefit other systems. For example, teaching clients capabilities to reduce parasuicidal behaviour not only decreases behavioural disturbance but may decrease emotional distress (e.g. the client no longer feels ashamed for engaging in the behaviour) and improve interpersonal functioning (e.g. absence of parasuicidal behaviour removes a cue for interpersonal conflict between client and spouse, decreasing the client's worries that her husband will leave her). All of these behavioural systems (affect, interpersonal, cognitive, sense of self, overt behaviours) are important in DBT. The affective system, however, is first among equals. Therefore, difficulties in affect regulation, theoretically, take prime position in comprehending the origins of BPD, along with the transaction between emotional vulnerability and invalidating environments (Point 5).

Inability to moderate affect

Drawing on the work of John Gottman and colleagues (Gottman & Katz, 1990), Linehan identified that clients with a BPD diagnosis have deficits in emotion modulation. Gottman and Katz identified four tasks in modulating ineffective emotions: (1) changing the arousal associated with the emotion; (2) reorienting attention; (3) inhibiting mood-dependent behaviour; and (4) organizing behaviour in the service of non-mood-dependent goals. Each successive task of emotion modulation requires more cognitive effort. Therefore, if clients are extremely emotionally aroused, strategies at the first level (modification of arousal) will more likely succeed than those at the highest level (organizing behaviour in the service of non-mood-dependent goals). Modification of arousal encompasses many standard cognitive-behavioural techniques. For example, using breathing or relaxation techniques can reduce the arousal in clients experiencing anxiety or anger. For clients with depressed mood behavioural activation can increase arousal appropriately. Reorientation of attention requires the client to distract from the stimulus generating the affect. All emotions have associated action urges that can maintain or even increase their intensity. Engaging in opposite to emotion action or behaviours incompatible with the mood-dependent action therefore assists in emotion modulation. For example, to manage anger towards her psychiatrist, a client who experiences urges to pace the room and shake her fist shouting loudly, might remain seated on her hands and speak more quietly. The client might also restructure her covert judgements about the psychiatrist by practising more validating statements about him (advanced acting opposite!). Clients with a BPD diagnosis frequently focus on organizing their activities around reducing their affect rather than on achieving key goals. For example, a client with panic disorder may arrange her day to reduce the likelihood of experiencing a panic attack, rather than attending college and doing the weekly shopping. Alternatively, the client who feels angry with her psychiatrist may focus on proving her point rather than working to ensure that she obtains the medication review she wanted. At this final and most complex level of emotion modulation, DBT therapists help clients to remain focused on problem solving and developing effective plans for achieving their goals. Part of these plans usually involves knowing and rehearsing the skills relevant to the other tasks in emotion modulation and helping the client to identify when to use each skill at each level.

As a consequence of clients' emotional vulnerability and difficulties in emotion modulation, DBT strongly emphasizes emotions within case conceptualization. DBT therapists particularly analyse how problematic behaviours may function to express or regulate affect. Without such an analysis more functional ways of expressing and managing emotions remain illusive. In analysing problematic behaviour, DBT therapists constantly assess the type, intensity and function of affect and help clients to find new, more skilful strategies for experiencing or regulating it (see Points 18–23).

5

Transactional theory of capability and motivational deficits

To explain the aetiology and maintenance of problematic behaviours associated with BPD, Linehan (1993a) proposed a transactional theory that combines biological, developmental and social research. She hypothesized that the problematic behaviours result from a dialectical transaction between a biologically based proclivity toward emotion dysregulation and an invalidating social environment(s). This hypothesis suggests that not only does the interaction of the individual's biology and social environment create the foundation for developing BPD, but also that the biology and environment reciprocally influence each other such that the emotional dysregulation creates a more invalidating environment and vice-versa. For example, a parent may become more invalidating over time in response to a temperamental child who is difficult to soothe. Linehan further proposed that these transactions result in a combination of capability and motivational deficits. More specifically, she suggested that individuals who meet criteria for BPD lack essential skills, including emotional regulation, impulse control, interpersonal and problem-solving skills and that internal and external factors both inhibit skilful behaviour and motivate problematic behaviour.

As part of the bio-social theory, Linehan (1993a) described how the emotion dysregulation experienced by borderline individuals results from a biologically based emotional vulnerability combined with insufficient emotion modulation capabilities. The greater emotional vulnerability increases the likelihood of emotions motivating maladaptive behaviour. Emotional vulnerability alone, however, would not lead to emotion dysregulation if the individual managed the emotions well. Unfortunately, borderline individuals also tend to lack the ability to manage their emotions. To identify specific capability deficits, Linehan has particularly incorporated the work of Gottman and Katz (1990), who have suggested that affect modulation requires the ability to: (a) change physiological arousal induced by the affect; (b) refocus attention away from the affective stimuli; (c) inhibit mood-dependent behaviour; and (d) organize one's actions to achieve a non-mood-dependent goal.

Though emotion dysregulation may cause some form of psychological problems by itself, only when such dysregulation transacts with an invalidating environment over a period of time does BPD develop. Linehan (1993a, p. 49) defined an invalidating environment as "one in which communication of private experiences is met by erratic, inappropriate and extreme response". Though borderline individuals usually first encounter invalidating environments during childhood, many find themselves in similar environments (e.g. marriages, treatment systems) during adulthood as well. Invalidating environments chronically reject or otherwise punish the individual's communication of private experiences (e.g. emotions, cognitions, action urges). Consequently, individuals learn to ignore or otherwise invalidate their own experiences and not to communicate them effectively. These environments also oversimplify the ease of solving problems and thus fail to teach individuals sufficient skills to regulate their own behaviour, tolerate distress or solve problems. Instead, these environments teach individuals to respond severely to any perceived failure. Finally, these environments intermittently reinforce the escalation of behaviours. For example, an invalidating environment may ignore expressions of distress until it leads to suicide attempts, substance dependence or bulimia and then intervene intensively. This intermittent reinforcement alternately motivates the individual to inhibit appropriate communications of internal experiences and requests for help on the one hand and to engage in extreme behaviours on the other.

6

Learning theory I: Classical conditioning

DBT is a cognitive-behavioural treatment based on *behavioural* theory rather than *cognitive* theory. In one conceptualization of the history of CBT, a focus on the principles of learning theory as a primary mechanism of change constituted the "first wave" of CBT, with a focus on cognition and its content forming the "second wave" (Hayes, Follette, & Linehan, 2004). "Third-wave" therapies, of which DBT was perhaps one of the first, possess a number of common features; re-examination of the applicability of learning theory to verbally mediated CBTs (in particular an emphasis on the function rather than the form of psychological phenomena), incorporation of mindfulness and acceptance into CBT and an emphasis on the relevance of the principles and procedures of the therapy to the therapist as well as the client (Hayes et al., 2004). DBT, like the original first-wave approaches, considers anything a person does—thinking and emoting as well as acting—as behaviour. Principles of learning theory apply equally to all of these aspects of behaviour. Therapists in DBT utilize these principles to assist clients to modify cognitions as well as emotions and overt behaviours. This Point, which focuses on classical conditioning, and the one that follows, on operant conditioning, discuss the application of learning theory in DBT.

Classical conditioning

Pavlov (1928/1995) first demonstrated the principles of classical conditioning in his now familiar experiments with salivating dogs. Pavlov showed that by pairing the sound of a bell (the conditioned stimulus) with the presence of food (unconditioned stimulus) over a number of repeated presentations, the bell alone could elicit salivation in the dogs (unconditioned response). This phenomenon, where the pairing of two stimuli results in one stimulus developing the capability of eliciting the response associated with the other stimulus, explains the development of a number of problems experienced by clients and forms the theoretical basis underpinning most treatments for anxiety disorders. These exposure-based treatments, discussed in Point 21, work by establishing a new learned association between the two initial stimuli.

Classical conditioning has illuminated the understanding and amelioration of trauma responses common among clients with BPD. For example, a client attacked in an alley (unconditioned stimulus) experiences anxiety whenever she sees alleyways or dark narrow streets and avoids walking in parts of her town with these features. In this example, the pairing of the conditioned stimulus, the alley, with the unconditioned response, panic, is overt and immediately comprehensible. In some circumstances, the association may be harder to discern and may be, at least initially, out of the client's awareness. For example, one client experienced flashbacks and anxiety in cafés, restaurants and hotels, although none of these venues were associated directly with a history of trauma. Initially, the therapist and client alike conceptualized the response to be a form of social anxiety triggered by uncertainties about the safety of the situation. On closer examination of the particular characteristics of the venues that elicited the anxiety response, compared to those that did not, the client and therapist identified that the smell of bacon, rather than social cues, elicited the anxiety response. The client then remembered that as a child the smell of bacon signalled that while her mother cooked breakfast, her stepfather had the opportunity to enter her bedroom and sexually assault her.

In both of the examples above the problematic affect for the client was anxiety. DBT applies classical conditioning principles to other emotions and to responses other than avoidance. For example, an adolescent client had a history of verbal and physical humiliation by his father following the usual behavioural peccadilloes of childhood. Intensely ashamed after such episodes, the boy frequently hid in a cupboard under the stairs. During community meetings on the adolescent in-patient unit where the client later received treatment, staff and clients' peers frequently provided feedback to clients about their behaviour. For this client, receiving feedback in the community meetings elicited intense shame, because of the history of pairing feedback about behaviour with humiliation. Furthermore, regardless of the valence of the feedback, the intensity of the shame resulted in the client experiencing second-person auditory hallucinations that criticized him for bringing himself to the attention of others and threatened to humiliate him further. In this example, the client experienced a shame response (unconditioned response) appropriate following extreme humiliation (unconditioned stimulus), but unwarranted in the current context of receiving feedback (conditioned stimulus).

7

Learning theory II: Operant conditioning

Operant conditioning refers to the circumstances in which the consequences of behaviour, intended or otherwise, affect the likelihood of whether the behaviour will occur again.[2] Reinforcing consequences are those that, on average, increase the likelihood that the behaviour preceding them will occur again, whereas punishing consequences are those that, on average, decrease the likelihood that the behaviour preceding them will occur again. Removal of reinforcing consequences of a behaviour also decreases the likelihood of the behaviour reoccurring. This latter process is known as extinction. DBT therapists utilize these principles of operant conditioning to understand the factors that maintain the client's problematic behaviours and prevent the use of more skilful behaviours. On the basis of this understanding DBT therapists then utilize contingency management procedures to change client behaviours (Point 22).

Effective use of operant principles relies on the therapist assessing and not assuming which consequences of a specific behaviour are reinforcing or punishing. Non-behaviourally trained, new DBT therapists frequently assume that a consequence is *a priori* a reinforcer or a punisher of a particular behaviour. For example, they might assume that praise reinforces all clients or that attention always reinforces parasuicidal behaviour. In actuality, only repeated analyses of behaviour can assist therapists and clients to determine whether a consequence reinforces, punishes or is unrelated to the behaviour.

---

2 A comprehensive explication of the principles of operant conditioning is beyond the scope of this book. Karen Pryor's (2002) *Don't Shoot the Dog*, provides an excellent explication of both the principles and their application.

35

When possible, therapists and clients manipulate the consequences and observe the impact on the behaviour to establish the contingent relationship between the consequences and the behaviour.

In assessing contingent relationships, there are two principles to which therapists must attend. First, the consequences that act to reinforce or punish behaviour may remain outside an individual's awareness and may bear little relationship to the stated intent of the behaviour. Second, both reinforcing and punitive consequences are often in play following any given behaviour. For example, a client takes a serious overdose with the stated intent of killing himself and escaping unbearable torment. This behaviour, however, has several consequences. Immediately the client takes the tablets, he begins to experience calmness and a release from his distress. Sometime later a friend finds the client and calls an ambulance, which transports the client to hospital. On admission to hospital, the client has his stomach pumped, has a drip inserted and is transferred to a medical ward where he receives a psychiatric evaluation. Some hours later, he receives a visit from his irate spouse, misses an appointment with his therapist and has his medication changed. All of these are consequences of the behaviour, but only the initial impact on the client's emotional state related to the client's stated intent of escaping his distress. Also, only some of the consequences affected the likelihood that the behaviour would occur again. In this case the powerful initial impact of decreasing emotional distress was sufficient to increase the likelihood of a reoccurrence (negative reinforcement), whereas the anger from his spouse, concern from his friend and the medical procedures decreased the likelihood of a reoccurrence (all examples of positive punishment). Whether any consequence reinforces or punishes behaviour depends on the client's learning history. For some clients the hospital admission, because it provides a temporary respite from current demands, increases the likelihood of more overdosing behaviour. Many therapists would consider the ride in the ambulance an irrelevant consequence, and for most clients it would be, but for one client an ambulance ride did reinforce overdosing. For him, the fast ride to hospital with the sirens blazing gave him a powerful sense of importance that was absent from the rest of his life.

Given the long-standing use of operant conditioning in CBT, it is pertinent to consider what makes its use in DBT distinctive. DBT applies these principles, first, to suicidal behaviours and, second, along with other "third-wave" therapies, to thoughts. For example, many clients experience a decrease in unpleasant affective states when they contemplate suicide, primarily because they believe suicide will result in a cessation of emotional pain. Thus, thinking suicidal thoughts is *negatively reinforced* by the removal of unpleasant affective states when the client thinks about dying (Shaw-Welch, 2005).

The identification of reinforcing consequences are an important component of functional analysis that endeavours to establish the purpose or function that a behaviour serves in the life of an individual. Functional analysis requires the identification of reinforcing consequences that maintain the behaviour (Iwata & Wordsell, 2005). DBT applies functional analysis to the suicidal, multi-diagnostic client and looks explicitly for commonality of function across apparently disparate problem behaviours. For example, a client with BPD and a comorbid eating disorder described a sequence of events in the previous week that resulted in her cutting her stomach and thighs repeatedly. The DBT therapist and client identified that a functional consequence of the cutting (out-of-session behaviour) was reducing shame elicited when the client saw herself in the mirror. Rehearsal of strategies for reducing shame associated with the client's body image then became the focus of the session. Reducing shame was also the function of another previously reported out-of-session behaviour, amphetamine abuse. During the course of the functional analysis, the client became mute, looked away from the therapist and rocked in her chair (in-session behaviours). The therapist hypothesized that the client was experiencing shame about aspects of her behaviour that made it difficult to share them with the therapist. Previous therapists had inadvertently negatively reinforced muteness and rocking in response to shame by changing the topic every time the client started to engage in these behaviours. Functional analyses of multiple targets (both in-session and out-of-session behaviours) enables DBT therapists to target solutions around common functions allowing for progress on multiple fronts simultaneously. This focus around commonality of function between current out-of-session targets, previous out-of-session targets, and in-session behaviours when they occur, results in some of the movement and flow in DBT sessions.

8

A behavioural approach to diagnosis

Linehan initially developed DBT for individuals who meet DSM-IV criteria for BPD (see Table 1).[3] The treatment conceptualizes these criteria behaviourally, i.e. the characteristics outlined in the diagnostic criteria are simply descriptions of behaviour. DBT's behavioural conceptualization of diagnosis flows from the radical behaviourist stance of the treatment that any response the organism makes (e.g. overt motor behaviour, thoughts, emotions and sensations) constitutes behaviour. Some of the DSM-IV criteria for BPD refer to overt behaviours, e.g. Table 1, criterion 4, impulsivity. Other criteria refer to covert behaviours of the client such as criterion 3, identity disturbance (American Psychiatric Association, 2000, p. 710).

Distinctively, DBT argues that the successful reduction or removal of the behaviours that constitute the diagnosis removes the diagnosis itself. A behavioural approach argues that: "A self or personality is at best a repertoire of behaviour imparted by an organized set of contingencies" (Skinner, 1974, p. 167). Thus, from a behavioural perspective, personality, and hence personality disorder, *is* only a series of overt and covert behaviours. All of these behaviours, overt and covert, are amenable to change using cognitive and behavioural principles and procedures (see Points 18–23). Once the behaviours change and the client neither displays the overt behaviours, nor experiences

---

3 Adolescents may be diagnosed with BPD provided the features have been present for longer than one year (DSM-IV). In practice many adolescent DBT programmes use summaries of the behavioural patterns described by the diagnosis rather than the diagnosis itself as inclusion criteria for the programme.

Table 1 DSM-IV diagnostic criteria for borderline personality disorder (BPD)

A pervasive pattern of instability of interpersonal relationships, self-image, and affects, and marked impulsivity beginning by early adulthood and present in a variety of contexts, as indicated by five (or more) of the following:

1   Frantic efforts to avoid real or imagined abandonment. (Do not include behaviors covered by criterion 5.)
2   A pattern of unstable and intense interpersonal relationships characterized by extremes of idealization and devaluation.
3   Identity disturbance: Markedly and persistently unstable self-image or sense of self.
4   Impulsivity in at least two areas that are potentially self-damaging (e.g. spending, sex, substance abuse, reckless driving, binge eating). (Do not include behaviors covered by criterion 5.)
5   Recurrent suicidal behavior, gestures or threats, or self-mutilating behavior.
6   Affective instability due to a marked reactivity of mood (e.g. intense episodic dysphoria, irritability, or anxiety usually lasting a few hours and only rarely more than a few days).
7   Chronic feelings of emptiness.
8   Inappropriate, intense anger or difficulty controlling anger (e.g. frequent displays of temper, constant anger, recurrent physical fights).
9   Transient, stress-related paranoid ideation or severe dissociative symptoms.

Source: American Psychiatric Association (2000). *Diagnostic and Statistical Manual of Mental Disorders (DSM-IV-TR)* (4th revised ed. text revision). Washington, DC: APA. Copyright © 2000 American Psychiatric Association. Reproduced by permission.

the covert behaviours (other than to a degree and intensity similar to the rest of the community) then the personality disorder is gone. This perspective contrasts with other theoretical models in which the idea of a personality disorder hinges conceptually on an "underlying personality organization" that causes the behavioural manifestations listed in the diagnostic criteria. In such models, curing the client requires changing the underlying personality organization.

Given the behavioural thrust of the treatment, the rationale for continuing to use a medical diagnostic system warrants explanation. As a treatment, DBT emphasizes effectiveness and as such strongly values empirical data. Currently, empirical investigation into the origins and maintenance of psychiatric disorders and the effectiveness of psychotherapy utilizes the diagnostic system. By using this system to anchor the phenomena DBT aims to treat, the treatment can access empirical literature in related fields and apply these findings directly to its understanding of the disorder and, more importantly, modify the treatment in the light of new developments. Using the extant diagnostic system has a further benefit, namely, many clients find validation and comfort from a diagnosis to describe their difficulties. There are, however, negative aspects to diagnosing clients. First, as many clients, and often clinicians too, believe that a personality disorder diagnosis describes an unchanging malfunction in an individual's personality, they naturally experience hopelessness in the face of the diagnosis. Indeed, given data from early studies on both the prognosis for clients with a borderline diagnosis and treatment outcome a degree of pessimism was understandable. This early pessimism has recently changed with the advent of effective treatments for BPD, of which DBT is one (see Point 30), and more recent studies of prognosis (Zanarini, Frankenberg, Hennen, & Silk, 2003). Second, clients and clinicians alike are concerned about the stigma attached to the diagnosis. While the outcome data on the efficacy of the treatment addresses some of the hopelessness of clients and clinicians, the behavioural conceptualization assists with both of these problems. By describing diagnosis as no more than behavioural patterns that the treatment targets and that are amenable to change, clients and clinicians can both remain hopeful, as well as focused on behaviours to change. For the client keen to avoid the stigma of a diagnosis, DBT offers a route to change those behaviours that frequently lead to stigmatization.

DBT strongly emphasizes enhancing clients' capabilities in a range of areas, including an understanding of both the diagnosis of BPD and the treatment's conceptualization of the diagnosis. Consequently, during assessment and pre-treatment, DBT therapists discuss the diagnostic criteria with the client, identifying which of the criteria the client meets. This discussion provides an opportunity for the therapist to assess the client's reactions to the diagnosis, to treat any problematic responses and to orient the client to the approach DBT takes to the treatment of the behaviours identified by the diagnosis.

9

Zen principles

The principles of Zen are observations about reality, which one learns en route to enlightenment. The principle that "the essential world of perfection is this very world" (Aitken, 1982, p. 63) most clearly expresses the essence of acceptance in Zen.[4] The world is perfect in the sense that it is the best that it can be. It cannot be any different than it is because it is created or caused by what has preceded it. Within this world, everything and every experience is impermanent, ebbing and flowing like waves. DBT therapists help clients to experience the world in these ways primarily by teaching the skills of mindfulness and radical acceptance. Acceptance again appears in the observations that: "All beings are the truth, just as they are" (Aitken, 1982, p. 6) and that all individuals have an inherent capacity for enlightenment. Therapists particularly use validation strategies and encourage clients to use "wise mind" and self-validation to accept themselves.

Zen also describes the consequences of not seeing and accepting reality. In his description of Zen, Aitken (1982) commented on the inherent nature of suffering and the effects of not accepting it: "The first truth enunciated by the Buddha is that life is suffering. Avoidance of suffering leads to worse suffering. . . . [W]e drink alcohol excessively to avoid that pain, thus causing more pain" (p. 49). Zen suggests that suffering results primarily from attachments to or insatiable desires for reality to be a certain way. These attachments or insatiable

---

4 This use of the term acceptance most closely resembles acknowledgement and does not imply approval or agreement.

desires have many forms, including a yearning for a particular relationship or for universal love, a desire for or attachment to a particular object, or an attachment to a set of beliefs or values. For example, therapists might have desires or beliefs about the way that they think their healthcare service should operate (e.g. the service should fund their programme). A strong desire or attachment to these beliefs may interfere with accepting reality as it is (e.g. the manager has an unlimited number of such requests and a very limited amount of funds) and responding effectively. When reality crashes into desire, the one with the driving desire receives the damage (e.g. intense anger, ruminating on judgements, increased stress). Zen does not state that attachments or desire should not occur; it simply highlights their relationship to suffering. It also suggests that one can reduce suffering by letting go of attachments or desires that obstruct seeing and accepting reality.

In addition to desires, "delusions" (i.e. cognitive biases or distortions) also interfere with accepting reality. For example, Zen proposes that boundaries are only a delusion and that all individuals and reality are actually one. Such a proposition provides an antithesis to the emphasis that many psychotherapies place on establishing boundaries. The following story, however, indicates the suffering that arbitrary boundaries can cause and suggests an effective means of removing such boundaries. Thich Nhat Hanh (1987) visited a friend with two young children and discussed life with a young family.

> Then Allen said, "I've discovered a way to have a lot more time. In the past, I used to look at my time as if it were divided into several parts. One part I reserved for Joey, another part was for Sue, another part to help with Ana, another part for household work. The time left over I considered my own.
>
> . . .
>
> But now I try not to divide time into parts anymore. I consider my time with Joey and Sue as my own time. When I

help Joey with his homework, I try to find ways of seeing his time as my own time. I go through his lesson with him, sharing his presence and finding ways to be interested in what we do during that time. The time for him becomes my own time.

. . .

The remarkable thing is that now I have unlimited time for myself!"

This story illustrates Yamada Roshi's point that: "The practice of Zen is forgetting the self in the act of uniting with something" (Aitken, 1982, p. 9). Thus, DBT validates a relational as well as an autonomous self and balances the traditional psychotherapy focus on developing and defining a sense of self with attention to developing a sense of connection to the world and letting go of arbitrary and ineffective boundaries.

DBT does not require therapists to practise Zen, but Zen practices of acceptance are critical to balancing the techniques of change in the treatment. Zen emphasizes experience and practice as means of understanding the world. The practice includes focusing on the current moment, seeing reality as it is without "delusions" and accepting reality without judgement. The practice also encourages students to let go of attachments that obstruct the path to enlightenment, to use skilful means and to find a middle way. In the early phases of learning or applying Zen, therapists often view it through the filter of a particular psychotherapy model or try to "bolt on" some of the practices. The following story illustrates the problems with these approaches and suggests an alternative path to learning.

Nan-in, a Zen master

received a university professor who came to inquire about Zen. Nan-in served tea. He poured his visitor's cup full, and then kept on pouring. The professor watched the overflow until he no longer could restrain himself. "It is overfull. No more will go in!" "Like this cup", Nan-in said, "you are full of your own opinions and speculations. How can I show you Zen unless you first empty your cup?"

(Reps & Senzaki, 1957)

This story about an overflowing cup applies equally well to learning about the other principles and practices of DBT. The journey of learning is never easy, but travelling without extra baggage will help.

Part 2

THE DISTINCTIVE PRACTICAL FEATURES OF DBT

10

Developing modalities to fulfil specific functions

The majority of psychotherapies, including most cognitive-behavioural treatments, consist of a single modality, for example individual psychotherapy or group psychotherapy. The single modality, however, may address multiple functions. In most therapy models, individual psychotherapy addresses motivational issues and psychological change and may attend to the generalization of treatment gains outside of therapy. DBT, in contrast, uniquely identifies five functions of treatment based on the motivational/capability deficit model of BPD (outlined in Point 4) and develops specific modalities to fulfil each function. Though any given modality within DBT may address more than one function, each function has its own dedicated modality. For example, individual therapy primarily works on improving motivation, but also attends somewhat to generalization. We describe each of the five functions which form a DBT programme.

Enhancing capabilities

Consequent upon their emotional vulnerability and early environmental experiences, clients with a BPD diagnosis have skills deficits in a number of areas, including emotion regulation, distress tolerance and interpersonal interactions. The treatment responds to these deficits by providing a modality dedicated to the acquisition of these basic capacities. Most frequently, DBT programmes deliver this function via skills training groups. The format of these groups may differ according to setting. For example, out-patient settings usually run one group per week of 2½ hours duration, whereas in-patient settings tend to provide frequent, shorter groups. All DBT skills groups follow a core curriculum (outlined in Linehan, 1993b). As this curriculum comprises part of an empirically validated package most programmes employ it in its entirety. Alternative or modified curricula may be utilized with other client groups (e.g. adolescents or learning disabled populations), provided that the primary function of skills acquisition remains the focus.

Enhancing motivation

To address factors impeding the client's motivation to engage in more skilful behaviour, DBT programmes most frequently develop the modality of individual DBT psychotherapy. Within this modality, comprehensive behavioural and solution analyses (Points 18 and 19) address the client's most problematic behaviours by identifying and treating the factors that interfere with the acquisition or implementation of more functional behaviours. During the solution analysis, the therapist utilizes the full panoply of cognitive-behavioural change procedures (Points 20–23), including exposure, contingency management and cognitive restructuring. Furthermore, for clients with a BPD diagnosis, sustaining the motivation to change presents a special challenge. Consequently, maintaining motivation to change during the therapeutic process requires continuous attention.

Ensuring generalization

As a cognitive-behavioural treatment, DBT recognizes that skills learnt in therapy do not automatically transfer from one environment (therapy) to another (clients' non-therapy life). Effecting this transition requires rigorous planning and frequent rehearsal. The intensity and lability of the clients' emotional responses frequently leads to significant environmental dependency in terms of skills utilization. For example, the client who can negotiate an interpersonal conflict successfully when emotionally calm may be at a loss for words in the presence of moderate affect. To compensate for this environmental dependency, DBT devotes an entire modality to generalization. In most of the empirically validated versions of the treatment telephone consultation fulfils this function (see Point 11). DBT teams may utilize other modalities applicable to their setting. For example, in-patient milieu staff may provide *in vivo* skills coaching to address problems on the unit as they arise. In applications of the treatment for clients dually diagnosed with BPD and substance dependence, DBT case managers may enter the clients' natural environments to provide coaching in specific skills (McMain, Sayrs, Dimeff, & Linehan, 2007).

Structuring the environment

Structuring the environment refers to both the treatment and non-treatment environments of clients. In terms of the latter, clients often live in environments that provide insufficient structure, support and validation. Additionally, these environments may reinforce inappropriate behaviours and punish more skilful behaviours. In some adaptations of the treatment, DBT therapists work alongside family members or social-care staff, assisting them to modify their own behaviour to promote the sustainability of changes that clients are making. For example, in DBT-A, an adapted form of the treatment for adolescents, parents attend skills training groups along with their adolescent children (Miller, Rathus, & Linehan, 2007). Dedicated family sessions may also take place to address specific problematic family interactions. Adult clients may also benefit from similar involvement from family members but such interventions rarely form a routine part of the intervention (Fruzzetti, Santisteban, & Hoffman, 2007).

In terms of structuring the treatment itself, delivering a five-function programme requires a degree of co-ordination within the system hosting the DBT programme. For example, all programmes need to initially acquire and subsequently maintain resources to deliver the programme and attend to the interaction or fit between the programme and the wider treatment system. Point 13 discusses this aspect of the treatment more fully.

Enhancing therapist capabilities and motivation to treat effectively

Last, but certainly not least, DBT programmes develop modalities to ensure that therapists acquire and implement the most effective treatment possible. Most DBT programmes address this function by holding a weekly therapists consultation meeting. DBT expects that therapists, of whatever experience and skill, require focused attention on this function each week. Working with clients experiencing significant emotional pain presents therapists with difficulties, especially when progress is slow, problems have endured for a long time and the clients' environments are resistant to modification. Therapists find remaining hopeful and in a therapeutic stance towards clients in such circumstances challenging. Continuing to adhere to a treatment active in the change process adds another layer of difficulty. Because of the immense difficulty of change and high levels of emotional distress, frequently intensified during therapy, clients often respond in ways that effectively punish the therapist for engaging in effective therapy. Most often, the client does not intend to punish the therapist; rather his or her behaviour results from wanting to reduce suffering in the moment. For example, a client experiences shame about her self-harming behaviour and the intensity of the affect leads to muteness when the therapist raises the topic. The therapist worries that continuing to focus on self-harm "shames" the client further and begins to avoid discussing self-harm. In the short term the client is relieved by the therapist's course of action, but she does not receive help in decreasing her self-harm or managing her shame more effectively. Point 29 discusses in more detail how the treatment tackles the therapist's therapy-interfering behaviour.

By focusing on therapist skill and capability and placing therapists' names on the agenda, the therapists' consultation meeting distinguishes itself from a case-discussion meeting. Each week, therapists raise problems they are experiencing in therapy to seek consultation from their colleagues. The team utilizes the principles within the treatment to both identify and solve presented problems and, as necessary, to treat the therapist to prevent burnout. Point 12 addresses this especially characteristic feature of the treatment. DBT programmes may also complement the consultation team with other modalities (e.g. individual supervision, training, staff incentives).

A DBT programme requires modalities to fulfil all five functions and, equally important, each modality within the programme must clearly link to its relevant function. In treatment services for clients with multiple problems and high levels of complexity, professionals commonly consider offering additional *ad hoc* interventions (e.g. phone contact or a skills group) in response to a crisis. In contrast, DBT distinctly offers co-ordinated and interconnected modalities. Activity in one modality, such as a skills group, receives further development and application in others, for example, individual psychotherapy and generalization. For example, skills training groups focus primarily on skills acquisition and a small amount of skills strengthening. The individual psychotherapist will focus on further strengthening the same skills during therapy sessions and planning for skills generalization. During generalization modalities, the same skill set is generalized to the non-therapy environments of the client. The primary DBT individual psychotherapist maintains an overview of all modalities. Characteristically, in a DBT programme the addition of new modalities only occurs when the team has clearly defined their function and established their relationship to the overall delivery of the treatment programme established. Random addition of treatment modalities is not a characteristic of DBT programmes!

11

Coaching on the phone

In contrast to most other psychotherapies, DBT requires that out-patient programmes offer a modality through which clients can access DBT providers outside of the clinical setting, when clients are in their natural environments. As a behavioural treatment, DBT emphasizes the need for such a modality to ensure learning will generalize beyond the therapeutic context. The treatment does not assume that skills practised in a clinical setting will automatically generalize to real-life settings. The context of applying skills may differ substantially from the context of learning skills, particularly in terms of the client's degree of emotional dysregulation and the environment's likelihood of providing a reinforcing response.

To facilitate generalization, DBT out-patient programmes generally provide clients with the opportunity to phone their individual therapist for brief coaching interventions between individual therapy sessions. During the telephone contact, the individual therapist offers skills coaching rather than psychotherapy or general support. The skills coach helps the client to generate, select and practise the appropriate skills needed to solve the most immediate problem. The skills coach does not analyse the problem in detail or discuss the client's longer-term problems. For example, if a client had strong urges to harm herself following an argument with her husband, she might phone the therapist for coaching on how to reduce those urges. When generating solutions, the therapist and client may consider interpersonal skills that would change how the client interacted with her husband in the immediate future. They would not discuss, however, all of the client's long-term marital problems. Indeed, for many clients ruminating on their long-term marital problems would have been a critical link in the chain between the argument and the self-harm urges. In such cases, the skills coach would suggest using mindfulness to decrease the ruminating.

If a client phones when highly suicidal, the therapist will try skills coaching to reduce the suicidal urges and to keep the client in an out-patient setting. In addition to skills coaching, however, the therapist may also need to use a variety of the interventions described in Linehan's suicide crisis protocol (Linehan, 1993a). If this combination of interventions does not reduce the suicidal urges and a risk assessment indicates that the client is at high risk for suicide, then the therapist would move to hospitalize the client or otherwise intervene in the environment to manage the risk.

To reduce the likelihood of clients associating suicide or other crises with more therapist availability, DBT therapists encourage clients to phone for skills coaching before they become suicidal or otherwise reach a crisis. For example, one client had a history of becoming suicidal in response to a variety of events that evoked shame. As a consequence of this initial shame the client would ruminate on all of the other things that she had done in her life that caused her to feel shame. As the shame increased, she would consider suicide as the only possible escape from the shame. Early in therapy, the client phoned the therapist only after the suicidal urges had begun. During individual therapy sessions, the therapist and client analysed solutions for the shame and rumination. To enhance the client's generalization of these solutions, the therapist encouraged the client to phone for coaching after trying to use skills for the initial shame and before beginning to ruminate. As the therapy progressed, the therapist also required the client to have tried more skills herself before phoning. This shaping of skills generalization decreased the likelihood of the client becoming dependent upon the therapist's coaching. To further prevent an association between crisis behaviours and therapist availability, most out-patient DBT programmes also have a rule that suspends access to phone consultation for 24 hours after an episode of parasuicidal behaviour. Notably, further analyses of the first randomized control trial comparing DBT to treatment-as-usual (Linehan & Heard, 1993) found that while a significant positive correlation occurred between frequency of parasuicidal behaviour and frequency of client phone calls with therapists in the treatment-as-usual condition, no significant correlation occurred in the DBT condition.

Although many therapists in the earliest stages of learning about DBT worry that clients will overwhelm them with telephone calls, therapists actually receiving supervision in DBT more frequently complain that clients do not call when encouraged to do so. A combination of factors may explain why clients generally do not overwhelm therapists with telephone calls. First, each therapist and client together determine the parameters of their telephone contact so that they can maximize the opportunities for generalization and minimize the likelihood of therapist burnout. Second, most clients attend to the therapist's limits with respect. Third, if a client violates the therapist's limits or engages in any other behaviour that decreases the therapist's motivation to provide telephone contact, the therapist treats the therapy-interfering behaviour. Examples of such therapy-interfering behaviours include the client phoning too late at night or too frequently, rejecting all of the therapist's suggestions or hanging up on the therapist. Finally, the emphasis on using the telephone to generalize skills rather than to provide general support leads to briefer phone calls and to clients learning to phone only when they are willing to work and not when they want only validation or soothing.

12

Consulting in a team

As described earlier, the consultation team primarily functions to treat professionals offering DBT by enhancing their capabilities and motivation to provide DBT as adherently as possible. DBT consultation meetings differ from traditional case meetings in the degree to which the meetings focus on the professional's problems in delivering the treatment rather than on the client's problems. An individual therapist or other DBT provider (e.g. skills trainer, skills coach in the milieu) might seek consultation for a variety of conceptualization or strategic problems, such as: "Have I missed any variables in my analysis?", "I don't know how to apply exposure in this situation", or "Does anyone have any other ideas about how to change this behaviour?" Alternatively, a therapist might need consultation for a motivational problem such as overwhelming or prolonged anger toward a client or strong urges to quit working with a client.

In response to these problems, therapists use many of the same strategies that they use with clients, particularly validation and problem solving. For example, to address the problem about exposure, the team might didactically review the basic principles of the procedure, help the therapist identify relevant cues to present or behaviours to block or role-play a scenario using exposure. For a more complex problem such as wanting to quit, other team members may apply the treatment, albeit briefly, to the therapist or prompt the therapist to do so. In one case, a behavioural analysis by the team revealed that whenever a particular client became passive during a session, the individual therapist began to think hopeless thoughts about whether the client would progress. These hopeless thoughts led to self-invalidating thoughts about the therapist's abilities and to guilt. The guilt led to the urge to quit treating the client. The therapist had tried cognitive restructuring for the hopeless thinking, but this intervention had not succeeded. The behavioural analysis itself helped the therapist to become more mindful of the relevant factors, but the consultation team also generated a number of specific interventions for these factors. To decrease the self-invalidation, they encouraged the therapist to mindfully describe her abilities. The more factual description revealed that she actually did need more skill to change the client's passivity effectively. The team then taught the therapist some additional techniques to minimize the client's passivity and role-played these with the therapist. This problem solving, combined with validation from the team, helped to ameliorate the therapist's guilt and, therefore, her urges to quit.

As in pre-treatment with clients, DBT requires consultation team members to make and maintain certain commitments. Most importantly, perhaps, members must commit to applying DBT as adherently as possible with clients. Members also agree to use the skills taught in DBT for themselves and to apply the therapy to themselves to solve problems in their DBT roles (e.g. consultation team member, individual therapist). Furthermore, DBT requires weekly participation at consultation team meetings. If a treatment provider stops attending weekly, the team would attempt to treat the consultation-interfering behaviour. If the behaviour persists, however, the provider should no longer say that he or she offers DBT. As discussed in greater detail below, team members also commit to a set of six consultation agreements. To strengthen these and any other commitments, the team utilizes the DBT commitment strategies.

To enhance team functioning, consultation team members adhere to a set of agreements that guide how the therapists interact with each other. When combined with the use of DBT skills, these agreements seem particularly useful in minimizing and resolving the types of conflict that often arise when groups of people work together. The agreements consist of the consistency, the consultation-to-the-patient, the dialectical, the fallibility, the observing-limits and the phenomenological empathy agreements (Linehan, 1993a). The phenomenological empathy agreement encourages team members to search for empathic, non-pejorative explanations for clients' behaviours. The dialectical agreement reminds the team to apply the dialectical philosophy, as discussed in Point 3. The agreement particularly emphasizes searching for syntheses to resolve tensions that arise between a therapist and a client or among team members. The consistency agreement states, in part, that all team members need not have a consistent response to a client. For example, a group skills trainer covering for an individual therapist on leave may hospitalize more quickly than the individual therapist would if the client threatens suicide. Such inconsistencies offer the client an opportunity to learn, with the therapist's coaching, how to cope with the inconsistencies and changes occurring outside of therapy. The fallibility agreement explicitly states that all therapists are fallible. This agreement functions to reduce the motivation to hide or minimize therapy problems because it assumes a priori that therapists have made mistakes and need consultation. If a team member appears defensive in response to receiving corrective feedback, the team might highlight this agreement and apply DBT strategies to help the therapist to accept the agreement.

The consultation-to-the-patient agreement states that DBT therapists do not act as intermediaries between clients and other professionals. Instead, DBT therapists coach clients on how to interact effectively with those professionals. Within the DBT team, for example, if a client has problems with the DBT skills trainer, the individual therapist would not complain to the skills trainer but might teach the client how to use interpersonal skills to change the skills trainer's behaviour and apply other CBT interventions to enhance the client's motivation to use existing skills. Though originally designed to counteract the passive yet demanding problem-solving style of BPD clients, the consultation-to-the-patient strategy also appears to decrease the likelihood of "splitting" among professionals. Such splitting tends to occur when professionals try to tell each other how to treat a client. This agreement removes that cause. As the agreement exists within the context of team members having committed to delivering the treatment adherently, members do provide constructive feedback if a therapist has failed to follow treatment principles or protocols. The team provides this feedback, however, to enhance the therapist's capabilities, not to mediate for the client.

The observing limits agreement requires that each therapist acknowledge and adhere to his or her own personal and professional limits and that other team members not judge these limits as too narrow or too broad. Observing one's limits might include agreeing to additional individual sessions when the client has received bad news or has skilfully requested them, not agreeing to re-schedule an appointment time for a client during a busy week, tolerating high suicidal risk in an out-patient setting rather than risk a reinforcing hospitalization or not tolerating a client screaming during sessions. This agreement, however, does not give therapists permission to break their commitments to providing adherent treatment. Neither does it give them permission to violate professional ethics. DBT also directs therapists to help clients to cope with difficult limits. For example, most therapists will not forego their vacations to meet with clients instead. Many clients, however, have substantial difficulties during these vacations. Depending on the specific anticipated difficulties, the therapist might offer an additional therapy session to help the client to develop a plan for this period, make audiotapes of coaching the client on skills or arrange for the client to meet with another DBT therapist during this period.

To further advance the team's effectiveness, DBT consultation teams have a rotating role of observer. Unlike other members who fully participate in the primary tasks of the consultation team, the observer notices the process of the team. The observer attends to whether the team has deviated from the treatment model and to whether team members have become unmindful or violated a consultation team agreement. He or she also notices if team members treat each other as fragile by avoiding difficult issues. The observer alerts the team to problematic processes to provide the team with the opportunity to change course. He or she may also highlight productive processes to fuel progress along a particular pathway.

13

Treating the system

Uniquely, DBT applies the treatment strategies utilized with patients to structure the treatment environment in which the DBT programme operates. In implementing a new psychotherapy or treatment programme, healthcare managers and therapists alike frequently assume that the organization planning to host the new development provides a relatively benign context for implementation. This assumption frequently proves to be false. Consistent with the research on implementation (Fixsen, Naoom, Blasé, Friedman, & Wallace, 2005), by identifying a specific function of "structuring the environment", DBT recognizes that successful implementation of treatment interventions requires organizational effort. Multi-function treatments, such as DBT, may require greater organizational effort and, because of their complexity, may be harder to implement with fidelity (Yeaton & Sechrest, 1981).

Just as clients benefit from a dedicated pre-treatment stage (Point 15) that identifies and matches their goals with those of the DBT programme, so an organization may benefit from a "pre-treatment stage" prior to implementation of a DBT programme. This Point discusses aspects of organizational pre-treatment, a particularly distinctive feature of DBT. Swales (in preparation) offers a more comprehensive discussion of the issues.

Organizational pre-treatment

Just as each DBT client requires a primary therapist responsible for delivering the individual psychotherapy component of the treatment and checking on other treatment modalities, DBT programmes require a "primary therapist" or "treatment champion" responsible for co-ordinating organizational pre-treatment. Programmes without identified champions tend to wither and die (Barwick et al., 2005). A senior clinician, administrator or manager may fulfil the role of treatment champion. This role requires the incumbent, during pre-treatment, to liaise with the organization, identify its goals and link these goals with those of the treatment programme. The champion also secures resources for the DBT programme, and, as implementation proceeds, ensures that the programme delivers the organization's goals. Most commonly, the champion is an interested clinician who becomes the leader of the DBT team if the organization commits to the implementation of a DBT programme.

In organizational pre-treatment, the team leader or champion, first, establishes the organization's goals with regard to clients with BPD. The leader asks whether the organization considers providing a psychotherapy service and treatment programme for clients with complex high-risk behaviours part of its remit. If yes, then the leader evaluates with the organization whether DBT can help the organization achieve its goals. DBT fits well into organizations seeking an evidence-based treatment for clients with a BPD diagnosis or suicidal behaviour or both; likewise, DBT is a good match for organizations wishing to introduce a systematic approach to the assessment and management of high-risk behaviours (Linehan, 1993a). For organizations concerned about high service utilization by the client group, DBT may prove more cost-effective than treatment-as-usual (Brazier et al., 2006). DBT also provides a co-ordinated team-based approach to a group of clients often considered as difficult to manage.

If the healthcare system planning the DBT programme does not consider the provision of psychotherapy for clients with BPD part of its remit, then implementation of DBT would be inappropriate. In some cases, however, clinicians in the healthcare system see DBT as a viable solution to organizational difficulties in treating the client group, but the organization remains unaware of the problems or conceptualizes them differently. For example, some organizations historically excluded clients with personality disorder diagnoses from mental health services, believing either that personality disorder was not within the purview of mental health services or that it was untreatable or both. In such organizations, clients with personality disorder diagnoses frequently remain undiagnosed but remain in the service treated for other problems. Clinicians know that they are treating personality disorder within the service yet managers remain ignorant of this fact and maintain that the service does not treat such clients. In these circumstances, the team leader assists the organization in identifying and analysing the problems observed by clinicians in order to clarify the organizational goals before proceeding to evaluate the appropriateness of DBT as a solution.

Following the identification of the organization's goals and of DBT as a match for these goals, the team leader then comprehensively orients the system to the requirements for programme delivery. The five-function structure of the treatment and its staged approach demands a considerable investment of personnel and time. The organization must anticipate an initial period of investment in training and skill development before any returns, in terms of its goals, become visible. To ensure the provision of the necessary resources (e.g. finance and time) for the implementation of the programme, the team leader shapes further commitment by the organization, utilizing all of the DBT commitment strategies.

During this process of organizational pre-treatment, identifying potentially incompatible organizational goals that have the capacity to interfere in effective implementation may prove useful in preventing problems during implementation. For example, the system may have a primary goal of reducing waiting times for treatment. Providing a long-term psychotherapy may interfere with achieving this goal if delivering the DBT service significantly decreases clinicians' time available for treating new referrals. As in pre-treatment with clients, resolving these tensions prior to beginning the programme may prevent difficulties in implementation. The team leader articulates the potential incompatibility of the organization's goals and utilizes the dialectical principles within the treatment to resolve any conflicts. The first step in this process is identifying the valid aspect of both goals. For example, wanting to provide timely generic services and a specialist psychotherapy service for clients with BPD are both valid goals. The team leader then works with the organization to consider whether providing a specialist service could also assist with reducing generic waiting times. For example, in some services, the absence of specialist psychotherapy programmes for clients with BPD results in high levels of consumption of generic resources. Offering a specialist BPD service may release some capacity within the generic service. If finding solutions to meet both goals proves unsuccessful, the team leader conducts a pros and cons analysis with the organization, to choose the goals that most accurately meet current organizational priorities. The decision taken may require that clinicians interested in implementing DBT radically accept that implementation will not occur at the present time.

During discussions with the organization and its representatives the team leader may experience pressure to compromise on the integrity of the DBT implementation in order to meet all of the organization's goals. Frequently, DBT teams in this circumstance opt for partial implementation, the efficacy of which remains uncertain. Using contingency management may prove helpful here. In the absence of the requisite resources to run the full treatment programme (e.g. time, training, finance and personnel) the team may decide not to implement any part of DBT until it has developed further the organization's commitment to comprehensive implementation. In other circumstances, delivering a small but highly adherent programme that delivers significant outcomes may prove useful in building organization commitment to develop further.

In addition to the pre-treatment strategies of goal identification and commitment, DBT clinicians practise mindfulness in relation to the organization and its representatives. Most importantly, therapists must uphold a non-judgemental stance, although this presents a challenge for most. Clinicians learn to respond non-judgementally towards their clients, and, with a little encouragement, towards themselves. Practising these skills in relation to the wider organizational system remains a novelty. Indeed therapists frequently reinforce each other for engaging in judgemental behaviour towards their employers. In some systems judgemental behaviour is *de rigeur*. Though judgemental responses to the system may provide immediate reinforcement for practitioners, the subsequent increased emotional arousal and reduction in problem-solving focus may lead to burnout. Also, judging the organization rarely assists it to change! Instead, DBT encourages clinicians and treatment champions to develop non-judgemental descriptions of factors that interfere with treatment delivery in the system, and to conduct behavioural and solution analyses of "organizational therapy-delivery-interfering behaviours". Therapists analyse these behaviours as they would the therapy-interfering behaviours of their clients. Effective implementation requires the development and implementation of thorough solution analyses for problematic links identified in behavioural analyses.

14

Structuring the treatment in stages

DBT conceptualizes the recovery of clients from BPD and associated comorbidities as following a series of stages. In the treatment manual Linehan (1993a) first described three stages of treatment; pre-treatment, Stage 1 and Stage 2. She has since added Stages 3 and 4 and described how a staged approach to treatment may apply to clients with problems other than BPD (Linehan, 1999). In this more recent thinking, clients may enter treatment at any stage, depending upon the severity and complexity of their difficulties. Following pre-treatment, which addresses assessment, orientation and commitment, clients with a BPD diagnosis enter Stage 1. This stage of treatment assists clients to achieve behavioural stability, by reducing threats to life and other severely destabilizing behaviours. After Stage 1, clients may progress through some or all of the remaining stages or decide to end treatment. Stage 2 focuses on emotionally processing the past and is especially relevant for clients with a past history of trauma. Stage 3 aims to assist clients to return to ordinary levels of happiness and unhappiness. Problems at this stage of treatment are of low to moderate severity and have only a moderate impact on clients' functioning, in comparison to Stage 1 and 2 problems. Stage 3 problems may include marital, education or employment difficulties. Stage 4 aims to enhance the capacity for joy and focuses on assisting individuals for whom ordinary happiness and unhappiness remains insufficient and who continue to experience a degree of meaninglessness or absence of connectedness. At this stage, long-term insight-oriented therapies may prove beneficial, as may spiritual or religious practices. The DBT therapist and treatment programme may work with clients through Stages 1 and 2, resources and expertise permitting. Publicly funded healthcare systems, in general, will rarely treat Stage 3 and 4 problems; rather private therapists and voluntary-sector organizations may provide services to address these difficulties. Orienting clients with BPD to Stages 3 and 4 of treatment may assist them in navigating the later stages of recovery.

Given the complexity and multiplicity of problems presented by clients with a BPD diagnosis, a staged approach to treatment orients clients and therapists alike to the order in which the treatment targets certain problems. Each stage of treatment has a particular goal, and treatment targets within that stage directly address the achievement of the goal. Thus far, DBT describes only the pre-treatment stage and Stage 1 in detail. Point 15 discusses pre-treatment further.

Stage 1: Achieving behavioural stability

During Stage 1, the therapist focuses on behaviours that pose direct threats to safety and stability in order to increase the client's immediate life expectancy, to decrease the frequency and intensity of seriously destabilizing and dysfunctional behaviours and to promote more effective connections with individuals and systems that support the client. In Stage 1 treatment, DBT therapists organize the treatment of clients' behaviours around a structured series of targets. First in priority are life-threatening behaviours (suicidal, parasuicidal, homicidal and other imminently life-threatening behaviours), followed by therapy-interfering behaviours and quality-of-life-interfering behaviours (see Point 16). The remainder of this book focuses on the structuring and execution of Stage 1. Cessation of suicidal and parasuicidal behaviours, for at least four months, with substantial reductions in urges to engage in these behaviours, significant reductions or complete elimination of major quality-of-life-interfering behaviours along with a notable increased use of skilful behaviour may prove useful markers to signal the end of Stage 1.

At the end of Stage 1, the therapist and client assess the client's remaining problems and establish the most appropriate treatment intervention depending on which stage of treatment is next most appropriate. DBT makes no explicit recommendations for any given treatment in subsequent stages, as this depends entirely on the difficulties that the client experiences. DBT does recommend, however, that therapists direct clients towards treatments that possess empirical evidence for effectiveness. Likewise, whether the client remains in treatment with his or her DBT therapist will depend upon the capability and capacity of the DBT therapist to offer the particular intervention or interventions required.

Stage 2: Emotionally processing the past

Stage 2 centres on emotionally processing the past. As many clients have a history of childhood trauma, this stage frequently focuses on the resolution and emotional processing of trauma memories. For clients without a history of trauma, Stage 2 may also focus on unresolved interpersonal or intrapersonal experiences associated with a BPD diagnosis that do not seriously destabilize the client. Such problems include a history of repeated loss and abandonment in childhood or serious interpersonal difficulties leading to frequent participation in unstable relationships. For clients with a trauma history and perhaps those without, progressing through an effective treatment at Stage 2 may prove necessary to ensure the continued maintenance of gains achieved in Stage 1. Otherwise, the client remains at risk of a return to Stage 1 behaviours to manage unbearable affect or intrusive cognitions.

The focus on first achieving stability before processing trauma was an especially noteworthy feature of DBT when Linehan first developed and evaluated the treatment. Until then, the therapeutic *zeitgeist* emphasized the processing of trauma as the first priority for clients with post-traumatic stress disorder (PTSD). Currently, most therapists would support

DBT's position of achieving behavioural stability prior to trauma processing, particularly when clients meet criteria for BPD and engage in suicidal behaviours. For these clients, commencing with trauma processing presents a recognized risk of increased suicidality, in the context of existing high risk, and further destabilization.

Transitions between Stages 1 and 2

DBT particularly attends to the contingencies that operate in the treatment system around the progression from Stage 1 to Stage 2. In healthcare systems under resource pressure and focused primarily on the management of risk, clients may face a reduction or withdrawal of resources as they become more stable. Some clients have frequently experienced this association of clinical progress with a withdrawal of therapeutic support. When faced with a removal of resources at the end of a successful Stage 1 treatment, clients with this history may become less motivated, decrease skill use and so deteriorate. In these circumstances, the withdrawal of therapeutic input punishes the client's use of skills. For other clients, the absence of treatment through Stage 2 results in deterioration. For example, most clients with PTSD require an exposure-based treatment following the successful completion of Stage 1. Failure to provide this treatment may leave the client struggling to manage ongoing symptoms of PTSD in the absence of therapeutic support. Over time, clients find this increasingly intolerable and may deteriorate. To counteract these problems, DBT programmes endeavour to ensure the maintenance of therapeutic intensity across the transition. If at all possible, an increase in clinical input as clients progress may prove helpful. Such an approach counteracts clients' learning histories that making progress leads to less support.

While encouraging programmes to reinforce clinical progress with either increased input or at the minimum maintaining current input, DBT therapists counterbalance this approach with an emphasis on withdrawing treatment at the end of the contracted period if the client has made insufficient progress. Making further or increased input contingent upon progress within DBT contradicts the approach of many mental-health interventions, which tend to provide more input in response to deterioration or absence of progress. Such stacking of the systemic contingencies to enhance clients' motivation, however, characterizes DBT. Also, continuing to provide an ineffective treatment could be considered unethical.

15

Strengthening commitment in pre-treatment

DBT pre-treatment is about helping the client make an informed, mindful choice about the DBT programme and increasing the client's committed behaviours. It is not about imposing the therapist's or system's commitment to having the client in the programme or even about talking the client into the programme. Paradoxically, to effectively connect the client to the treatment, the therapist must remain willing to let the client go.

During pre-treatment, individual therapists focus on accomplishing a series of tasks to prepare clients for the entire DBT programme. These tasks include identifying the clients' treatment goals and assessing the corresponding problems, orienting the clients to DBT, strengthening their commitment to participating in the programme and developing the therapy relationship. This initial stage usually requires from three to six sessions.

Though many clients easily identify appropriate treatment goals, some clients struggle with this task. A behavioural analysis of the struggle may reveal that the client never learned how to identify goals, lives in an environment that does not encourage goal setting, fears that others will ridicule existing goals or believes that any attempt to reach existing goals will end in failure. After learning about the obstacles that interfere with the client identifying goals, the therapist would try to remove these obstacles with a variety of interventions. For example, if a fear of how others will respond interferes, the therapist may employ a combination of mindfulness, cognitive restructuring, interpersonal effectiveness and exposure to help the client overcome the fear and set treatment goals.

To orient the client to the various components and pro-cedures of a DBT programme, therapists utilize a variety of treatment strategies. Didactic strategies efficiently provide a substantial amount of necessary information. Therapists often utilize these strategies to inform clients about the treatment modalities, stages and targets, the bio-social theory, a selection of strategies and any programme rules. Didactic strategies cannot communicate, however, the experience of participating in DBT. Metaphors often better convey this sense. For example, one therapist frequently compares participating in DBT to working with a personal trainer at the gym. The work will be challenging and often painful, progress will be slow, hope will come and go, but reasons not to attend will always exist, and receiving a massage will always seem preferable. Ultimately, the most effective way for the client to gain a sense of the treatment is for the therapist to apply the treatment procedures during the pre-treatment stage. For example, if the client fails to attend a pre-treatment session, the therapist may challenge the client about the behaviour, conduct a behavioural analysis and request the client to rehearse skills relevant to preventing the behaviour. In one case, an assessment of past treatments revealed that the client left a previous treatment following an unmet demand for more therapeutic time. The client believed that the therapist refused the demand as a result of not understanding her needs. Based on this information, the DBT therapist clarified the contingencies in DBT that could lead to more time (or less), helped the client to consider alternative interpretations of the refusal and rehearsed how the client could effectively inform the DBT therapist about any similar interpretations or urges to terminate treatment.

To strengthen the client's commitment, the therapist employs a variety of specific techniques. These include evaluating pros and cons, shaping the commitment, connecting present commit-ments to prior commitments, highlighting the freedom to choose and the absence of alternatives, playing devil's advocate and using a combination of "foot-in-the-door" and "door-in-the-face". "Foot-in-the door" refers to the technique of obtaining a small commitment and then asking for a larger one, while "door-in-the-face" refers to the opposite technique of asking for a large commitment and then settling for a smaller one. Social psychology research (Goldman, 1986) has suggested that these techniques work best in combination. Playing devil's advocate, a procedure developed by Goldfried (Goldfried, Linehan, & Smith, 1978), requires the therapist to argue against making a commitment, while the client argues in favour of it. Once the client has rehearsed arguing in favour of committing, the therapist reinforces this behaviour by relinquishing the negative side and agreeing with the client. In highlighting the freedom to choose/absence of alternatives, the therapist highlights both the choices that a client can make and the limitations of those choices. For example, a client has the freedom to commit to the DBT programme or not but cannot commit only to certain modalities within the programme. The final decision remains with the client, but each decision has consequences. For example, in response to any problem, clients can choose to solve the problem, change how they respond to the problem or remain miserable. Remaining miserable is a viable option, but not an option that requires any time and attention from the therapist.

As in other therapies, the therapy relationship also develops during pre-treatment. The client's motivation to participate in the therapy is enhanced by a number of strategies that continue throughout the treatment. The validation and reciprocal strategies offer the most obvious choices for strengthening the relationship. The therapist can validate the wisdom of the client's long-term goals, the functions of target behaviours, the difficulties of changing those behaviours and discussing them with a stranger, and the decision to commit to DBT. Though necessary in the development of the therapy relationship, the acceptance strategies are not sufficient in the application of the treatment as a whole. DBT therapists in training, however, sometimes struggle with how simultaneously to apply the treatment fully and to develop the relationship. Usually this occurs because they assume that the acceptance strategies, such as validation and warmth, will enhance the relationship, while change strategies, such as problem solving and confrontation, will harm it. Such an approach creates two important problems. First, clients cannot make informed commitments to the treatment if they have not had the opportunity to experience some of the change strategies during pre-treatment. Second, delaying the introduction of problem-solving strategies until after the development of the therapy relationship also delays the assistance that clients need to decrease their emotional suffering and achieve their goals. Often, the most validating thing that a therapist can do is to help a client solve the problem(s) leading to the suffering, rather than simply empathizing with the suffering. In most professional relationships, individuals are more likely to maintain relationships with those professionals that help them solve problems effectively.

Though some of the pre-treatment tasks logically precede others (identifying goals and orienting before obtaining a commitment), therapists generally interweave the tasks across the pre-treatment sessions. Therapy might begin with a discussion of the client's treatment goals. During this discussion, however, the therapist could listen for opportunities to orient the client to the treatment. For example, if the client identifies "having better relationships" as a goal, the therapist might tell the client about the interpersonal-effectiveness skills and describe how they will address problems in the therapy relationship and therapy-interfering behaviours. The therapist could also weave in strengthening the client's commitment to any of those goals. While working on these tasks, the therapist would also attend to cultivating the therapy relationship. After identifying the goals, the therapist could orient the client to the target hierarchy by linking the targets to the client's goals and then assess the most important target behaviours. While discussing these targets, the therapist would weave in obtaining a commitment to the target hierarchy and perhaps assess this commitment by asking the client to begin completing the diary card. Assessing the history of the target behaviours may also provide an opportunity to describe the bio-social theory. The therapist could then orient the client to other important aspects of the treatment. Throughout this orientation, the therapist would continue to interweave commitment strategies and cultivating the relationship. Finally, the therapist would review whether the client had made the necessary commitment to the treatment and utilize the commitment-strengthening strategies to enhance the commitment further.

16

Targeting behaviours according to a hierarchy

DBT addresses the complexity and multiplicity of clients' problems by organizing treatment around a hierarchical list of treatment targets, referred to as the target hierarchy. The treatment utilizes the target hierarchy in two main ways. First, the hierarchy lists, in order of importance, the primary treatment targets for Stage 1, providing a method for coherently addressing the extensive comorbidity in this client population. Structuring the treatment around targets also allows for the systematic management of high-risk behaviours such as parasuicide or serious aggression. The organization of the hierarchy with the riskiest behaviours at the top ensures that therapist and client regularly review and, more importantly, directly treat these behaviours. During pre-treatment, the DBT individual therapist works with the client to link these treatment targets to the client's overall goals for treatment. Second, the target hierarchy guides the session agenda and thus determines the structure and focus of any given session or interaction with the client. Effective targeting also reduces confusion and lack of clarity over direction and assists the therapist to remain focused during each session.

Organizing primary targets

DBT organizes the primary targets in order of priority as follows: decreasing *life-threatening behaviours*, *therapy-interfering behaviour*, and *quality-of-life-interfering behaviours* and increasing *behavioural skills*. Reducing the first three groups of targets by increasing behavioural skills forms the overall plan for the first stage of treatment. This Point discusses the top three groups of targets. Point 20 describes behavioural skills.

The top category of targets originally included only suicidal and parasuicidal behaviours, although Linehan recognized that other targets, such as homicidal behaviours in forensic settings, may become the first focus (Linehan, 1993a). As the treatment has been adapted and applied in a wider range of settings than originally envisaged, Linehan renamed this first target group *life-threatening behaviours* and expanded it to encompass the following:

- Suicidal behaviours
  — Parasuicidal behaviours
- Homicidal behaviours
- Threats to engage in any of the above
- Urges to engage in any of the above
- Significant changes in suicidal/homicidal ideation
- Other imminently life-threatening behaviours

For each client, the therapist identifies in pre-treatment which *specific* behaviours the client engages in within each of these categories. Occasionally, the inclusion of parasuicidal behaviours in this top category causes novice DBT therapists some conceptual difficulty. Kreitman (1977) used the term "parasuicide" to describe two groups of behaviours: first, non-fatal, intentional, self-injurious behaviour that resulted in actual tissue damage, illness, or risk of death; second, ingestion of drugs or other non-prescribed substances or in excess of prescription with clear intent to cause bodily harm or death. Whether any given instance of parasuicidal behaviour imminently threatens the life of the client, and regardless of any conscious intent of the client to die, parasuicidal behaviour is the strongest predictor of suicide. Indeed, clients with a BPD diagnosis who engage in parasuicidal behaviour are twice as likely to die by suicide as clients with the diagnosis who do not (Frances, Fyer, & Clarkin, 1986). Thus, DBT includes these behaviours within the first category of targets. Failing to attend to parasuicidal behaviours consistently can inadvertently communicate that the therapist believes the behaviour is inevitable and unchangeable or that the behaviour is safe. The rigorous, even relentless, attention to life-threatening behaviours is an especially distinctive feature of DBT (Linehan, 1993a, p. 174).

Next, DBT targets behaviours that interfere in the progress of the therapy. Although even the earliest texts on cognitive-behavioural treatments (e.g. Beck, Rush, Shaw, & Emery, 1979), emphasized the importance of a collaborative relationship, DBT was the first cognitive-behavioural treatment to articulate a clear structure for tackling problems in the therapeutic alliance. Under the rubric of *therapy-interfering behaviours*, the client and therapist identify any behaviour in which either party engage that interferes with effective therapy. Common types of client behaviours include non-attending behaviours (e.g. missing sessions, coming late to therapy), non-collaborative behaviours (e.g. not practising homework, saying frequently "that won't work", remaining mute in sessions) and behaviours that demotivate the therapist (e.g. invalidating the therapist's efforts to help, verbally abusing the therapist). Based on previous experiences of therapy, the therapist and client may know in advance the likelihood of their respective specific therapy-interfering behaviours occurring in DBT. Of course unanticipated problems in the alliance frequently occur. The DBT therapist will highlight these behaviours for the client as they occur and add them to the hierarchy, as appropriate.

Common therapist therapy-interfering behaviours result from a non-optimal dialectical stance, such as extreme rigidity or flexibility, or an imbalance of validation and confrontation. Novice DBT therapists commonly interfere with therapy by failing to apply the treatment model in its entirety, preferring to utilize only those aspects of the treatment with which they are most familiar or most comfortable. Addressing therapist therapy-interfering behaviour of whatever type, an especially characteristic feature of the treatment, requires a willingness on the part of the therapists to change their problematic behaviour (see Point 30). The consultation team supervises therapists and helps them identify and solve therapy-interfering behaviours. Discussing their own therapy-interfering behaviours with clients also provides an opportunity for therapists to model, in a non-defensive manner, how to solve difficulties in therapy and in relationships more generally.

Quality-of-life-interfering behaviours denote behaviours that cause serious and severe destabilization of the client. Overall DBT aims to improve the quality of clients' lives substantially; achieving stabilization forms the first step in building a more functional quality of life. At this point in the target hierarchy, the treatment addresses those behaviours associated with other psychiatric diagnoses. Thus, DBT explicitly anticipates and plans to treat the complexity and multiplicity of disorders presented by clients with a diagnosis of BPD. For example, a client diagnosed with BPD also met criteria for PTSD, bulimia nervosa and depression. In constructing her targets under *quality-of-life*, the therapist focused on those features of the diagnostic profile that caused maximal destabilization in the present. In this case, these were:

PTSD	Dissociation
Bulimia nervosa	Bingeing
	Vomiting
Depression	Depressed mood

In a forensic setting, a client met criteria for antisocial personality disorder (ASPD), substance misuse and PTSD, as well as BPD. For him, the quality-of-life behaviours targeted were as follows:

ASPD	Destruction of property
	Verbal aggression
Substance misuse	Cocaine use
PTSD	Flashbacks

As this client also had a history of convictions for grievous bodily harm, the treatment targeted this behaviour and associated urges under the top target of life-threatening behaviour.

In addition to behaviours associated with other psychiatric diagnoses, at this point in the hierarchy the therapist and the client target any other client behaviours that seriously destabilize his or her life, for example seeking frequent psychiatric hospitalizations, forming or maintaining seriously abusive relationships or forensic behaviours. Retaining a balance between addressing the complexity of the client's problems and not overwhelming either the client or the therapist with too many targets remains important here. With too many behaviours on the target list the therapist continues to face the problem of determining which behaviour to target in any given session.

Structuring the session agenda

In addition to targets forming the overall plan of attack for the treatment programme, they also constitute the hierarchy of targets for the individual psychotherapy component of the treatment. To utilize the target hierarchy for its primary purpose of keeping a clear focus in the session, the therapist must know whether the client has engaged in any of the target behaviours since the last appointment. Therefore, as in most cognitive-behavioural treatments, DBT requires clients to regularly self-monitor their top targets in treatment. Clients use a diary card for the purpose of self-monitoring. At the start of each session the therapist requests and reviews the diary card and uses the information on the card, along with the client's target hierarchy, to select the target for the session.

Without a diary card, a session cannot proceed as the therapist does not know the appropriate target for treatment that week. If the client presents without the diary card, completing the card becomes the first task of the session. The therapist may then move to solve the problems leading to non-completion of the card. Resolving difficulties with self-monitoring can prove a surprisingly important task in therapy, as the difficulties that clients experience with self-monitoring frequently provides insight into their approach to problems in general. For example, clients may avoid facing difficulties because they experience critical thoughts and become over-whelmed with shame about their behaviour. Alternatively, clients may experience hopeless thoughts about changing their behaviour and intense sadness. In assisting the client to solve these problems as they arise in completing the diary card, the DBT therapist also highlights how the client may solve similar problems when they arise outside therapy.

Targets in other modalities

DBT distinctively organizes interactions between therapist and client within each modality of the treatment around a clearly specified behavioural hierarchy. The particular set and order of targets within each modality flows directly from the multi-functionality of the treatment (Point 11). For example, in skills training groups the target hierarchy prioritizes *skills acquisition*. Only if clients engage in *behaviours likely to destroy therapy* will the group skills trainers divert from teaching skills. In practice such behaviours occur only rarely. After teaching new skills, DBT skills groups target *therapy-interfering behaviour* (e.g. non-completion of homework, non-participation in group discussion, dissociation). Thus, skills training groups reverse the ordering of behavioural skills enhancement and therapy-interfering behaviour compared to individual therapy. In practice, the group skills trainers mostly ignore therapy-interfering behaviours occurring in group. If these behaviours become sufficiently problematic the individual therapist may address them in the individual modality. This re-ordering of targets results in a major shift in the style of the skills group. DBT skills training groups resemble more closely an evening class or college course than a psychotherapy group, with the group skills trainer functioning more as a teacher than a therapist.

The group skills trainers do remain awake to managing the group process but they do not discuss the process of the group within the group.

17

Validating in the current context or clients' inherent capabilities

Validation strategies provide the counterpoint to the problem-solving strategies (see Points 18–23) and together these two sets of strategies form the heart of DBT. In validating the client, the therapist identifies and confirms veridical aspects of the client's emotional responses, thoughts, behaviours and goals. Validation strongly contrasts with clients' self-invalidation and historical and current environmental invalidation, in which others in their environment dismiss aspects of the clients' responses as inaccurate or inappropriate. DBT assumes that within all aspects of the clients' functioning—no matter how dysfunctional to the outside observer—a component of the response is wise, functional and makes sense, i.e. is valid. The client's goals, past history or current environmental context may provide reasons for validation. For example, parasuicidal behaviour may be the only strategy that the client has learnt to decrease extreme negative affect; as such parasuicide is valid in terms of both the client's past learning history and current goal to decrease emotional arousal. If a client lives in an environment that only responds to legitimate demands for attention and care when the client harms herself, then parasuicidal behaviour becomes a valid means of obtaining care in that particular environment. The therapist works with the client to distinguish the valid aspects of any behaviour from the invalid. For example, parasuicidal behaviour has validity with respect to a short-term goal of reducing affect but not with respect to a long-term goal of becoming more stable and in control.

DBT therapists utilize validation strategically to fulfil five different functions: (1) to balance change with acceptance; (2) to strengthen clinical progress; (3) to strengthen self-validation; (4) to strengthen the therapeutic relationship; and (5) to provide feedback to the client about their responses. The primary function of validation is to balance change. When Linehan was developing the treatment, she observed that the incessant focus on change presented a major challenge to clients, often leading to treatment drop-out. She hypothesized that a constant focus on change when there are so many problems both overwhelms the client and invalidates his or her belief that he or she is incapable of change. Linehan recognized the importance of introducing a strong focus on acceptance into the treatment to address these difficulties. Surrounding the intense focus on problem solving with validation assists the client to manage the distress elicited by the strong push for change. While the primary reason for incorporating validation into the treatment was to balance change, any validating response of the therapist may fulfil additional functions simultaneously. For example, a client reports an argument with a family member in which he or she became angry and out of control, throwing an object at the family member. The client says, "It was appalling—I shouldn't have behaved that way". In response the therapist may say, "You're right. This was not your shining moment!" This response provides feedback to the client about his or her response during the argument and verifies his or her perception that throwing the object was a problem. The therapist's honesty, when combined with his or her non-judgemental approach to the client, also strengthens the therapeutic relationship. The response of the therapist in this scenario also illustrates the difference between validation and positive feedback. Validation does not require the therapist to be positive, rather the therapist conveys which aspects of the client's responses are accurate, regardless of whether they are positive or negative.

While validation is common in any psychotherapeutic approach, and, indeed, can be the basis of an entire approach (as in Rogerian psychotherapy; Rogers, 1951), three aspects of validation are especially distinctive in DBT. First, DBT actively seeks to find the validity within clients' responses. Second, DBT articulates six levels of validation, of which the final two are especially distinctive. Finally, DBT describes two types of validation; explicit verbal validation and implicit functional validation.

The active searching for validity in the client's responses contrasts with many CBT approaches, which, while using validation and acceptance strategies, focus more on identifying and modifying dysfunction. DBT also challenges dysfunction but emphasizes equally the validity of responses along with the necessity for change. For example, a client, in the context of an unsuccessful attempt at skill use, reported the cognition, "I am hopeless at everything I try". While the therapist invalidated the component of the statement that the client was "hopeless", as would any traditional CBT therapist, the DBT therapist also validated that the client was accurate in her perception that she had frequently experienced failure in attempting new strategies to solve problems. The therapist then went on to analyse in detail why the attempt at the new skill had been unsuccessful and developed a plan with the client to resolve the obstacles to implementing the skill. By moving to validate the client's perception that she frequently failed, the therapist avoided an argument with the client about the relative frequency of success in trying new activities.

Linehan (1997) described six levels of validation. Other therapeutic models use the first four of these levels: (1) staying awake; (2) accurate reflection; (3) articulating unverbalized thoughts or emotions—mind reading; and (4) validating in terms of the client's past history or biological dysfunction. The final two levels—validating in terms of (5) the present context; and (6) radical genuineness—are especially distinctive in DBT. When validating in terms of the present context, the therapist identifies the client's response as a "normal" reaction in the situation, in other words, anyone would respond in the same way. As a consequence of extensive histories of invalidation, clients often believe either that all aspects of their responses are inaccurate or they are profoundly confused about which responses are valid and which invalid. Level 5 validation assists clients to begin to determine which aspects of their responses make sense in terms of population norms. Returning to the example above, in learning more of the context of the argument and discovering that the family member was highly critical of the client, the therapist may say, "It makes sense to me that you were angry, everyone experiences anger when criticized". Present context validation helps clients counteract self-invalidation and thus reduces arousal in the moment, helping the client to continue with the therapy. This level of validation does not preclude the therapist from conveying the invalid aspects of the behavioural response. For example, throwing an object at a family member is invalid if the client hopes that his or her family members will respond to him or her as someone who is more in control of him- or herself.

Level 6 validation is termed radical genuineness. When using this strategy the therapist conveys his or her genuine human response to the client; he or she does not treat the client as fragile but rather like a robust individual who can hear the truth. Level 6 validation requires the capacity on the part of the therapist to respond to the client as a fellow human being rather than as a client. DBT invites therapists to respond to their clients as they would to a family member or friend who reported the same events or emotional responses. The example above, when the therapist said that the aggressive outburst in the context of an argument was not his or her best moment, is an example of a radically genuine response to the client's behaviour. The therapist can also be radically genuine in his or her response to the client's circumstances. For example, the client reports that her only friend is leaving the area. The therapist might say, "You must be totally devastated and wondering how you are going to manage". For the response to be maximally effective, radical genuineness usually rests on effective Level 3 validation (mind reading) and knowing the client's history. The therapist's own personal style will also determine the form of the response. Naturally, there are as many ways of conveying radical genuineness as there are therapists and most therapists new to the treatment have to practise being more of themselves (how they are in their non-therapist roles) with their clients. Therapists frequently find this strategy difficult as they have spent many years perfecting their role as therapist, which, among other things, provides a degree of distance from clients. Consequently, therapists may worry about the personal impact of decreasing the degree of distance between themselves and the client. Remembering that radical genuineness is a therapeutic strategy proves helpful for concerned therapists. The strategy does not prescribe abandoning the professional role towards the client altogether as to do so would be at the least ineffective and at the worst unethical. Rather, the strategy asks that the therapist, at a moment when it would be helpful to the client, treats him or her as they would other individuals in their life and not as a fragile client.

Finally, DBT describes two types of validation; explicit verbal validation, as described above by the six levels, and implicit functional validation. In functional validation, the therapist does not verbally validate the wisdom or accuracy of the client's response, rather it is with actions that he or she communicates validity. For example, a client in session reports a major problem. Rather than saying to the client, "You're right that is a major problem. I can understand why you would be worried about it" (explicit verbal validation), the therapist moves in immediately to problem-solve. In doing so, the therapist functionally validates the verisimilitude of the client's statement. In using implicit functional validation, the treatment highlights a paradox (see Point 24 on dialectical strategies) that sometimes the most validating response to a client's dilemma is to help them to solve it.

18

Analysing behaviours, with a twist or two

DBT views the problem-solving strategies as the core set of strategies for changing target behaviours, and these strategies provide the predominant substance of a session. Within a session, the problem-solving strategies assess the antecedents and consequences of the target behaviour and apply behavioural principles of learning to identify the variables that elicit and maintain the behaviour. Furthermore, problem-solving strategies apply empirically supported interventions to treat the problematic behaviour, integrate multiple CBT procedures as solutions and apply those solutions within the session. Problem solving can be divided roughly into two interconnected components: (1) a behavioural analysis that assesses the variables controlling the target behaviour; and (2) a solution analysis that generates and implements more effective behaviours.

A behavioural analysis enables individual therapists to assess variables that elicit and maintain a problematic behaviour in the current context. It focuses on variables immediately preceding and following the behaviour, or on the present rather than the distant past. In addition to the traditional emphasis on identifying the function of behaviours, behavioural analyses in DBT also pay particular attention to affective variables. The most distinctive feature of this procedure in DBT, however, may be its application to in-session behaviours, as well as out-of-session behaviours. After describing the various components of the analysis as they relate to both in-session and out-of-session, we will present a more extensive clinical example of each type.

A behavioural analysis requires the therapist to define a specific behaviour, conduct a chain analysis of that behaviour, and identify the function and any other controlling variables through pattern recognition and hypothesis testing guided by the treatment's theories. To behaviourally define a problem for treatment, the therapist and client must formulate the problem in terms of the client's behaviour, not in terms of judgements, interpretations, status or another individual's behaviour. "Unemployed", for example, refers to a general status that may result from behaviours such as failing to apply for a job, disclosing too much personal information during an initial interview, repeatedly arriving late for work or yelling at the boss. Defining and describing a specific behaviour seems especially important when addressing in-session behaviours. For example, many clients have experienced healthcare providers referring to them as manipulative or suggesting that they want to sabotage a treatment. Both "manipulative" and "sabotage" describe possible intents or functions of behaviours rather than any actual behaviour. Actual behaviours that may lead others to assume sabotage include clients repeatedly missing sessions, refusing to answer questions in sessions or increasing self-harm after the therapist has highlighted progress on that behaviour. When behaviours are confused with their functions, the comprehensiveness and accuracy of the behavioural analyses decreases because assumptions are made without assessment. A more comprehensive analysis might reveal that a client wants the treatment to work but becomes so ashamed when discussing her behaviour that she avoids the session to avoid the shame, not to sabotage the treatment. Furthermore, behavioural definitions that include inaccurate interpretations or judgements will more likely elicit negative responses from clients, as they would from most people.

After defining the target behaviour, the therapist and client complete a chain analysis of that behaviour. Together they assess in moment-by-moment detail everything that the client experienced or did, from the environmental event that prompted the behaviour through to the consequences of the behaviour. This chain provides the necessary information for gaining insight into the variables that contributed to an episode of the target behaviour. As critical as a detailed analysis and insight are, however, the therapist must remember that they only provide the foundation on which to build the solution analysis later and are not the primary mechanisms of change themselves. A therapist will deliver a more adherent session with a briefer chain analysis interwoven with a thorough solution analysis than with a lengthy chain analysis and abbreviated solution analysis.

The following scenario provides an example of a chain analysis of an overdose of sleeping tablets. A client asked her husband to spend more time with her. His refusal led to an argument and the husband's departure. After he left, the client remained judgemental of her husband, and her anger remained high. Suddenly she noticed that she was alone. She then had a strong sense of loneliness. Following this sense, the client had the thoughts that her husband would never return and, "I can't cope with being alone". These thoughts elicited fear, which she scored initially as a 3 on a 5-point scale. The client then began to think, "I can't cope. I'm going to go crazy. I've got to escape". The client now scored her fear as a 5 and her panic as a 3. She then thought, "What can I do? I could take some pills". Her fear immediately decreased to a 3 and her panic to a 1. She promptly took half of a bottle of sleeping tablets. Upon swallowing them, her fear decreased to 1 and the panic disappeared. She became semi-conscious. Later, her husband found her and rushed her to the hospital, where they pumped her stomach and admitted her to a psychiatric unit. During her stay in the hospital, the nurses were very validating, and her husband visited her often and apologized profusely for having left during their argument. The client enjoyed her husband's visits, though she did feel some shame about her behaviour.

While obtaining a moment-by-moment account of the antecedents, the behaviour and the consequences through the chain analysis, the therapist will attempt to identify those variables that control the behaviour. The therapist will highlight potentially important links and recognize patterns of behaviour within and across analyses. Furthermore, the therapist will generate hypotheses based on the bio-social and behavioural theories about causal relationships among links. When in doubt as to which links have the greatest impact, the bio-social theory would suggest attending to the affective links, such as the anger and the fear in the example above. In this case, the fear, along with the related panic, was identified as the most important variable in controlling the suicidal behaviour. Without them, the behaviour would not have occurred. A solution analysis would generate specific solutions for the anxiety and panic and may also generate interventions for those variables (e.g. many of the cognitions) that elicit or exacerbate the emotions. In contrast, the anger contributed only indirectly to the suicidal behaviour by increasing the client's arousal and making her more emotionally sensitive and reactive to whatever followed.

Behavioural theory emphasizes attending particularly to those variables related to the function(s) of the behaviour. The client above overdosed with the intent of escaping from intense fear and panic, and the behaviour achieved this objective. Research (Linehan, Comtois, Brown, Heard, & Wagner, 2006a) on the reported intent of parasuicidal behaviour among borderline clients suggests that the behaviour frequently functions to provide emotional relief. Often, though, behaviour serves more than one function, and clients may remain unaware of other functions beyond their conscious intent. In the above example, the client did not expect the nurses to validate her, nor her husband to visit and apologize; she had expected to die, after all. This couple, however, had a pattern of fighting, overdosing and re-engaging, such that overdosing increased the time spent with her husband more effectively than directly asking him to do so. Over time, the husband's more attentive response to the client following parasuicidal behaviour had developed into a secondary function of the behaviour outside of the couple's awareness. A thorough solution analysis should address both primary and secondary functions of the behaviour.

When conducting a behavioural analysis, it helps to remain cognizant of the many factors that might interfere with the progress of the analysis. Emotion dysregulation and invalidation of self-constructs interfere with the cognitive processes required to learn and solve problems. Research (Kremers, Spinhoven, & Van der Does, 2004) has also revealed that as a consequence of comorbid depression, individuals meeting criteria for BPD tend to have poor autobiographical memories, another important component of problem solving. Similarly, several studies (e.g. Jones et al., 1999) have highlighted the prevalence of dissociation among BPD subjects. If such factors significantly interfere with the progress of analysing an out-of-session behaviour or if the session behaviour also occurs in chains leading to the out-of-session behaviour, the therapist may temporarily pause the analysis of the out-of-session behaviour and analyse the in-session behaviour instead.

The following clinical vignette summarizes the behavioural analysis of an episode of dissociation that occurred during a session while analysing an episode of binge eating. After assessing the antecedents of the binge, the therapist asked the client to describe the binge itself. At this point, the client dissociated, preventing any further progress in treatment. The therapist helped the client "re-associate" and then conducted a brief analysis of the dissociation. The client reported that as soon as the therapist had asked and she had begun to think about what she had eaten, she had a strong emotion of shame. She felt her face flush and started judging herself as "disgusting" and "useless", which further increased her shame. When the therapist repeated the question, the client thought, "I can't tell her or she'll hate me", and then became quite fearful that either the therapist would hate her for not answering the question or for what she had eaten. Dissociation then occurred in response to the high anxiety. Though commonly viewed as a classically conditioned response to anxiety, dissociation in this client seemed to respond to operant conditioning as well. The therapist hypothesized that the client's history of healthcare providers reducing demands and removing the client from stressful situations in response to dissociation may have contributed to this episode of the behaviour. Therefore, the solution analysis attended to both aspects of learning. The therapist and client also recognized a pattern from other analyses in which shame led quickly to anxiety about the response of others. Because of this pattern, they decided to address the shame in the solution analysis as well.

19

Integrating multiple CBT procedures in a solution analysis

The solution analysis aims to change those variables that currently control problematic behaviour. Perhaps the most distinctive feature of this analysis in DBT is the way in which multiple CBT procedures are interwoven throughout the solution analysis. DBT particularly employs skills training, exposure, contingency management and cognitive restructuring. Critical to the success of integrating these interventions is the use of the behavioural theory to match specific solutions to specific problems. If the client does not have the requisite skills to solve the problem, the client's individual therapist would teach the necessary skills. Alternatively if skilful behaviour in the client's repertoire is inhibited by unwarranted emotions, then the therapist would apply exposure therapy. If the skilful behaviour has been either punished or not reinforced in the client's environment or problematic behaviour has been reinforced, the therapist would apply contingency management. Finally, if maladaptive cognitions interfere with skilful behaviour, then the therapist would use cognitive modification. Of course, a skills trainer might view one solution as a skill, while a cognitive therapist would view the same solution as cognitive restructuring. Similarly, one behaviourist might argue that an intervention works because it changes the contingencies, whereas another behaviourist could argue that the intervention works because of exposure. Though DBT emphasizes using theory to guide the selection of solutions, it focuses on the effectiveness of the respective positions rather than endorsing any position as right.

Attending to the dialectical principles, the solution analysis should also reflect a balance of acceptance and change. In one case, a client felt extreme guilt for having caused her parents significant stress as a consequence of her drug addiction. She believed that her parents' problems were all her fault and that she ought to die. The suicidal urges functioned primarily to decrease the guilt. In this case, the therapist and client accepted at least some of the guilt as a warranted emotion. They generated solutions to increase tolerance of the guilt (e.g. finding meaning, radical acceptance) and to repair the damage to her parents (e.g. helping her parents more, using more skills to maintain sobriety). The therapist and client decided, however, to change the "all my fault" with traditional cognitive restructuring. They also challenged the "ought to die" thought by highlighting how much more stress this would cause the parents and by hypothesizing that the thought functioned to give the client permission to try to escape from the guilt.

Generating solutions

A solution analysis has three basic steps: generating, evaluating and implementing solutions. The first step, generating solutions, requires the therapist and client to identify as many potential solutions as possible for each relevant link in the chain analysis. The therapist integrates various CBT interventions as appropriate without becoming overly focused on or attached to any one intervention. For example, novice therapists often focus almost exclusively on skills or skills plus cognitive restructuring as solutions, but a solution analysis that considers only skills provides only a quarter of the solutions available. Similarly, many clients initially demonstrate a tendency to overly rely on the distress tolerance skills, rather than use the full range of skills.

Solution generation itself presents a problem for many clients with BPD. As a result of developing in an invalidating environment, some clients never received adequate modelling of how to generate solutions. Other clients have acquired the basics of solution generation but the behaviour remains weak or inhibited because in the past their solutions have failed, been ridiculed or otherwise punished. For example, when a client suggested higher education as a way to improve her quality of life, her less-educated parents responded by asking, "Who do you think you are? Do you think that you are better than us?" Linehan (1993a) has suggested that clients with BPD also have a tendency to generate solutions that require someone else (e.g. therapists, social services, family) to solve the problem for them. In one case, the client's only proposed solution to his drinking problem was to ask his psychiatrist for medication. Another patient's only suggested solution to forgetting therapy appointments was to ask staff to remind him. DBT would treat these problems associated with solution generation just as it would treat any other therapy-interfering behaviour.

Evaluating solutions

After generating solutions, the therapist and client must evaluate the potential efficacy of the various solutions. The evaluation should also identify potential obstacles to implementing solutions. Like suicidal clients (Williams & Pollock, 2000), clients with BPD seem to emphasize the potential negative outcomes of solutions. Though this emphasis may result from an information-processing bias, the client's expectations may also result from an actual lack of skills related to the solution, the anticipation or experience of extreme affect, or the fact that the client's natural environment will punish or at least not reward adaptive solutions. DBT therapists would again use CBT interventions to remove these obstacles. For example, two clients each stated that validation of another person "won't work" as an interpersonal solution and refused to use the skill. Analyses of the "won't work" and subsequent refusal, however, revealed two very different reasons for the in-session behaviours and required very different solutions. In the first case, the therapist suggested that they rehearse validation anyway to better assess why it wouldn't work. This rehearsal immediately revealed that although the client used validating words the tone sounded patronizing. The therapist then helped the client to strengthen this skill so that it would succeed. A brief chain analysis in the second case revealed that the client immediately had the thought, "He doesn't deserve validation", when the therapist suggested that the client validate her husband. The therapist highlighted the judgement and suggested mindfulness (specifically, being non-judgemental and focusing on effectiveness) as a solution, but the client refused to practise this skill. A further analysis revealed that the client maintained the judgements because they provided her with self-validation. The therapist and client then rehearsed other ways for the client to validate herself without judging her husband or being ineffective. After this, the client stopped objecting to validation as a solution.

Implementing solutions

Finally, the client and therapist select a set of solutions and then implement those solutions. We cannot over emphasize the importance of this step occurring during the session. The therapist cannot achieve adherence if solution implementation does not occur in the session! If the solutions include new or difficult skills, the client rehearses those skills during the session. This rehearsal strengthens the skills, challenges the client's expectations of failure, and allows the therapist and client to identify and solve problems that might interfere with the successful implementation of the skills outside of therapy. If the solutions include any of the other CBT interventions, the therapist conducts the appropriate procedures during the session. DBT generally interweaves these procedures informally into the treatment rather than following the more structured formats of traditional CBTs. For example, if a client avoided asking the therapist for help because the client feared that the therapist would respond with rejection, exposure would probably serve as the primary intervention. Prior to the exposure, however, some interpersonal skills training might increase the likelihood that the client would ask for help in a way that the therapist could reinforce, while a cognitive modification of expectations might increase the client's collaboration with the exposure procedure. Finally, the therapist would reinforce the client's appropriate request for help.

Clinical vignette

The first behavioural analysis described in the last Point offers an opportunity to illustrate how a therapist and client may interweave multiple solutions for a single episode of behaviour. To enhance the clarity of the illustrations, we will present each solution analysis in the chronological order of its corresponding chain analysis, rather than in the order of solution generation in the session. Also, the solutions identified for the parasuicidal behaviour represent a summary of the solutions generated over several analyses of similar episodes of the same behaviour.

In the first case described above, the therapist encouraged interpersonal effectiveness skills as a solution to increase the likelihood that the client's husband would agree to spend time with her when she initially asks. Though his refusal to spend more time with her was not directly linked to her increased suicidality in this chain, the behavioural analysis did reveal a reinforcing link between the parasuicidal behaviour and the husband's behaviour. One way to change this contingency was to increase the time with the husband in response to the client being interpersonally skilful. The judgements and anger that followed the husband's departure were not key variables in this chain, but the therapist encouraged the client to become mindful whenever judgements occurred. Over time, the client also learned various emotion-regulation skills for the anger. Indeed, she eventually generated validating thoughts about her husband's wish to spend time with his friends as a way to act opposite to her emotional urges.

In response to the loneliness, a common link across chains, the therapist and client generated a variety of solutions, some of which helped in the short term and others that created longer-term change. Initially, the client generated a list of distractions to cope with being alone. The use of these skills reduced the likelihood of the loneliness leading to intense anxiety in the moment, but they did not change the client's general relationship to loneliness over time. The client also succeeded in changing the associations with being alone (the cue that prompted the loneliness) by learning to consider being alone as an opportunity to do things at home that her husband did not enjoy. This solution decreased the likelihood of loneliness, but again it did not change the experience of loneliness itself. Teaching the client how to experience the loneliness mindfully and how to develop a sense of connection to the universe at large proved the most effective solutions for the loneliness. Cognitive restructuring decreased the worry that the husband would not return but it had little impact on the "can't cope" thoughts or the subsequent fear.

To treat the fear, which provided the primary motivation for the overdose, the therapist suggested a combination of mind-fulness and emotion-regulation skills. This combination of both allowing and decreasing the fear seemed critical to reducing the parasuicidal behaviour. First, the client practised mindfully describing the "I can't" thoughts and refocusing her attention on the task at hand. Next the client identified the action urges elicited by the anxiety (e.g. more "I can't" thoughts, taking pills) and developed a plan to act opposite to these urges (e.g. asking, "What skills do I need to use?" and throwing away the pills). The therapist also encouraged the client to phone her for skills coaching. Longer-term solutions included implementing exposure procedures for the cue of loneliness and working on increasing mastery in other areas of her life.

If the client's anxiety increased beyond a certain level or panic had begun, she would become cognitively dysregulated and require additional skills or adaptations of skills. Attending to Gottman's tasks of emotion regulation and their corresponding cognitive requirements (Gottman & Katz, 1990), the therapist suggested that the client use grounding and distraction in response to high levels of fear and panic and then progress to the other solutions. Also, reviewing notes helped to overcome the memory problems associated with cognitive dysregulation. For example, during a session, the client could easily list negative consequences of self-harm as a way to inhibit her urges, but she had great difficulty recalling them while panicking. To solve this obstacle, she kept a detailed list of negative consequences in front of her medication.

To address the reinforcing consequences of the overdose, the therapist also employed contingency management. The treatment could not prevent overdosing from decreasing fear (thus the emphasis on treating the fear with other interventions), but it did succeed in extinguishing the secondary reinforcement of the husband's post-parasuicidal increase in attentiveness. Meeting with the client and husband together, the therapist developed a plan to change the husband's behaviour such that he became more attentive when the client engaged in interpersonally skilful behaviour and less attentive when she engaged in suicidal behaviour.

20

Using skilful means

A major theoretical underpinning of DBT's conceptualization of BPD is that as a result of the combination of emotional vulnerability and invalidating environments clients have skills deficits (Point 5). DBT utilizes the different modalities of treatment to achieve the three key tasks in skills training: skill acquisition, skill strengthening and skill generalization. DBT skills groups focus primarily on skills acquisition and a degree of skills strengthening. Within the individual therapy component, the therapist strengthens skills by identifying opportunities to utilize either new or weak skills, rehearsing those skills with the client and tailoring them to the client's particular circumstances. Generalization modalities focus on ensuring that skills learnt or strengthened in therapy transfer to the client's non-therapy environment.

To become more skilful, clients must learn both acceptance- and change-based skills (Linehan, 1993b). DBT teaches four groups of skills balanced on this dialectic, with mindfulness and distress-tolerance skills on the acceptance end and interpersonal effectiveness and emotion regulation on the change end. Effective use of all of the skills depends to a degree on mastery of mindfulness. Therefore, the mindfulness module is taught at the start of each of the other three modules, and each of these other modules contains skills based on the mindfulness component (e.g. mindfulness of the current emotion in the emotion-regulation module).

Two of the skills-training modules heavily emphasize traditional cognitive-behavioural skills. The interpersonal effectiveness module draws on long-standing work in assertiveness and social skills training. Standard cognitive-behavioural procedures for dealing with a range of problematic emotions form the basis of the emotion-regulation module, for example, the role of cognition modification in reducing and changing emotions. In addition, the module emphasizes the role of opposite-to-emotion action in the moderation of unwarranted affects. Acting in accordance with the action urge of an emotion plays as crucial a role in the onset and maintenance of an affect as cognition does. Thus acting opposite to the urge will decrease the intensity of the affect. Acting opposite to the action urge forms part of all established CBT treatments for anxiety and anger. DBT applies the same principle to the treatment of other affects that are unwarranted (e.g. shame, guilt, sadness).

The distress-tolerance module combines skills from standard crisis intervention approaches with aspects of Zen practice, in particular *radical acceptance*. Radical acceptance encourages the comprehensive acceptance of, and engagement with, the facts of the present moment and is based on the assumption that suffering arises from the combination of pain and the non-acceptance of the pain, i.e. a statement that whatever is occurring "should not" be happening. Radical acceptance requires a relinquishing of the "should" and movement towards engaging effectively with whatever is occurring in the present moment. For example, an adolescent client frequently became annoyed with her parents for restricting her freedom to go out with her friends at the weekend. The client complained bitterly to her therapist about her parents' behaviour, saying that her parents "should" just stop worrying, as she had not harmed herself for some weeks, and let her have as much freedom as she wanted. The therapist encouraged the client to practise radical acceptance. In these circumstances, there were several aspects of the situation to radically accept: first, that in this moment her parents remained highly anxious about her; second, that this was a natural consequence of the client's long history of suicidal and self-harming behaviours (often precipitated by interpersonal conflict with friends); and, finally, that only more time without future self-harm would reassure the client's parents. While the client found practising radical acceptance difficult, she observed that using the skill reduced her dysregulation towards her parents and her suffering when she was required to remain at home.

When it was first developed, DBT distinguished itself from mainstream cognitive-behavioural treatment by teaching mindfulness, a set of skills derived from Zen Buddhism. At around the same time Jon Kabat-Zinn (1991) was utilizing mindfulness in the treatment of physical conditions in his treatment programme Mindfulness-Based Stress Reduction (MBSR). Since the advent of MBSR and DBT, incorporating mindfulness into psychological treatments has become more frequent and increasingly is considered as a vital component of many psychological treatments (Hayes, Follette, & Linehan, 2004).

Mindfulness is the process of paying attention with intention to the experience of the moment. DBT introduces clients to seven skills to assist in the development of mindfulness. The first of these is *Wise Mind*, a state of mind characterized by the integration of emotion mind and reasonable mind. The experience of *Wise Mind* combines a sense not only of intellectual knowledge but also of intuitive wisdom. The practising of six further mindfulness skills facilitates access to *Wise Mind*. DBT teaches three types of practice, or *what* skills: *observing*, *describing* and *participating*. Each of these practices are engaged in *non-judgementally*, *one-mindfully* and *effectively* (the *how* skills).

In contrast to other mindfulness-based treatments that teach the acquisition of mindfulness primarily via extended experiential learning practices, DBT initially teaches mindfulness skills in a more didactic way through shorter practices, which often have a distinct focus. For example, an early practice in MBSR and Mindfulness-Based Cognitive Therapy (MBCT) might be a 45-minute body scan, whereas in DBT an early practice might be 3 minutes listening to sounds. Indeed, MBSR, and its derivative MBCT, would be wary of considering mindfulness as a skill at all, as to do so runs the risk of seeing mindfulness as a "doing" activity rather than as a mode of "being" (Williams & Swales, 2004). Initially DBT both teaches mindfulness as an activity "to do" and then strengthens and generalizes the skill, thus helping clients to develop a different way "to be".

Linehan introduced *describing* as a separate skill to assist individuals with a borderline diagnosis in the difficult task of *observing*. In contrast, Zen practice explicitly discourages describing or putting words to the observed experience, nor is it a feature of other mindfulness-based therapies, which emphasize *observing*, where the task is simply to notice the contents of experience. Though neither Zen nor other mindfulness-based treatments include *describing* as part of the practice itself, students or clients have a dialogue with a teacher or therapist to reflect on their observing. Thus, describing experiences forms part of the process of developing mindfulness. Because of the potential that adding words will distort the observing of an experience (e.g. by adding interpretations or making assumptions), however, caution is advised in the use of words, keeping the description as close to the direct observation as possible.

While other mindfulness treatments such as MBSR and MBCT primarily teach *observing* and use *describing* as a means to explore experience, DBT uniquely emphasizes teaching *participating*. Clients and therapists practise full participation in the moment by letting go of *observing* and *describing* and becoming one with what they are doing. Consistent with the essence of Zen, the goal of DBT is to participate fully, non-judgementally and effectively in one's life.

The *how* skills, *non-judgementally*, *one-mindfully* and *effectively*, describe the manner in which to conduct each practice. Mindfulness requires letting go of value judgements (e.g. good, bad, should, should not, ought and ought not). Judging adds constructs to an observed experience and results in the observer reacting to these constructs rather than reality. The major difficulty for therapists and clients alike with judging is that it often increases the intensity of affect in problematic ways.

DBT invites clients and therapists to practise non-judgemental thought and action both as a means of responding more directly to the world and of preventing needless exacerbation of emotion. Being mindful requires doing one thing at a time and focusing attention completely on the task at hand. The practise of acting *one-mindfully* helps clients to remain focused on the present moment and to let go of ruminating about the past or worrying about the future. Bringing attention in this way to the present moment can enhance awareness of the richness of experience, or highlight previously unnoticed aspects of frequently occurring events. Finally, mindfulness encourages the individual to focus on effectiveness. Rather than becoming caught in judgements of good versus bad, DBT therapists and clients practise doing what works in any given situation.

The skills group teaches the basics of mindfulness as a skill and the individual therapist strengthens the client's capacity and motivation to become more mindful. For example, during a discussion of events leading up to an episode of self-cutting, a client became very self-critical and judgemental about herself, which demotivated her from participating in the session. In treating the decrease in motivation, the therapist first helped the client to notice that she had become judgemental and then to rehearse simply observing the judgements without becoming caught in them. The therapist also highlighted the judgemental voice tone that the client initially used to notice the judgements and shaped the client in using a more matter-of-fact tone. Being mindful in this way enabled the client to participate once again in the session.

Frequently, multiple skills are relevant in solving the problematic links in a behavioural analysis. For example, following an argument with her sister over household chores, a client experienced intense anger and verbally insulted her sister. Immediately afterwards, she judged herself for losing her temper and withdrew to her room overwhelmed with shame. She subsequently took an overdose that temporarily relieved her shame and led to a reconciliation with her sister. In this

115

sequence of events, as part of a comprehensive solution analysis, the therapist assisted the client with interpersonal skills to more effectively engage in negotiations with her sister over household chores (DEAR MAN and GIVE skills; Linehan, 1993b). From the emotion-regulation module, acting opposite to the action urges associated with anger (verbally insulting her sister) and shame (hiding in her room) helped to decrease the intensity of the unwarranted emotions. As part of the shame response was warranted (verbal abuse was contrary to the client's values), the client also rehearsed apologizing to her sister for the insult (acting opposite to justified shame). As the negative judgements she had made about losing her temper had exacerbated her shame response, the therapist encouraged the client to mindfully observe the negative judgements. Finally, from the distress-tolerance module, the therapist had the client rehearse the pros and cons of the client's decision to overdose as a solution to emotional distress and interpersonal conflict. Early in therapy, therapist and client may only have time to rehearse one or two of these skills in any one session. As the client becomes more familiar with the skills, and briefer rehearsal is required, a wider variety of skills can be woven into a single behavioural analysis.

21

Exposing to a variety of affects

DBT employs exposure procedures when clients engage in maladaptive behaviours as a consequence of unwarranted emotions (i.e. not based on the objective facts of the current situation). Distinguishing it from traditional exposure therapies that focus on fear, DBT applies exposure procedures to the full range of emotions (e.g. shame, anger, sadness and joy) that become causal links leading to target behaviours. For example, one client experienced extreme shame (i.e. beyond what the comments warranted) any time her husband commented negatively about any aspect of her appearance. The client then either purged or severely restricted her food consumption to decrease the shame. Although the client's individual therapist included other solutions in the analysis (e.g. mindfulness of negative judgements, challenging of negative assumptions, interpersonal skills to change the husband's comments) these solutions had a limited impact because of the severity of the shame. Using exposure to desensitize the client to the husband's comments proved critical. As expected, the exposure procedures directly decreased the client's shame response and her subsequent eating-disorder behaviour. As an additional benefit, the decrease in shame also increased the client's ability to use other skills.

To test this expansion of using exposure to treat other emotions, a recent pilot study by Rizvi and Linehan (2005) investigated the efficacy of exposure-based procedures in the treatment of shame. Using a single-subject design with five suicidal women who met criteria for BPD, the first author saw each subject for an 8–10 week exposure-based intervention. The results revealed a significant decrease in the average intensity of shame experienced across clients between pre- and post-treatment. Though the authors acknowledge the need for a larger, controlled, trial the results of this pilot study support extending the use of exposure to the treatment of shame at least.

DBT also differs from traditional exposure therapies in the frequency with which it uses exposure to treat problematic in-session behaviour. In one case, the client had learned in previous treatments to associate praise of progress in treatment with the treatment ending before she had achieved her goals. Therefore, when her DBT therapist praised or highlighted any progress, the client would become frightened of treatment ending and would besiege the therapist with a tirade of other problems. Because the contingencies in DBT differed from those of previous treatments, the fear was unwarranted. To decrease the client's fear in response to praise, the therapist used exposure. In another case, a behavioural analysis of a client's refusal to complete her diary card at the beginning of the session revealed that when she looked at the diary card and thought about her drug abuse, she experienced an overwhelming sense of sadness. Though the drug abuse justified some amount of sadness, the intensity was unjustified and interfered with the treatment. To decrease the emotion and therapy-interfering behaviour, the therapist exposed the client to the questions on the diary card until the client had completed the diary card and the sadness had subsided.

Regardless of the specific context or emotion requiring exposure, DBT therapists apply and teach clients to apply the standard procedures of exposure treatment (e.g. Barlow, 1988; Foa & Rothbaum, 1998). The therapist or client must present the cue or conditioned stimulus that elicits the emotion, and the client must experience the emotion as it rises and falls. The therapist or client also must prevent or block any maladaptive overt or covert action tendencies associated with the emotion (e.g. prevent attacks associated with anger, escape resulting from fear or hiding associated with shame).

In one case, whenever the therapist announced an impending trip, the client experienced overwhelming sadness. The associated action tendencies included thinking, "Everyone leaves me. Nobody cares about me", tears, a notable increase in phone calls to the therapist prior to the departure and occasionally suicidal threats. Using exposure as one of the solutions to this set of problems, the therapist repeatedly presented the cue by reminding the client of the trip and discussing what the client would do during that time. The therapist also encouraged the client to act opposite to the behavioural urges resulting from the intense sadness and directly blocked those behaviours herself whenever possible. She particularly had to remain careful not to reinforce any of the behaviours, particularly by reassuring the client in response to the tears or by changing the trip in response to the suicidal threats. Like many clients, this client benefited from using other skills, particularly mindfulness, during the exposure. For example, she learned to remain more mindful of her cognitions rather than escalate the sadness even higher by ruminating on everyone who had ever left her. Such ruminations would be the equivalent of someone with a spider phobia handling a spider that started giving birth to a dozen more spiders.

Complicating the analyses, many clients have emotional responses to other emotions. Some clients become afraid or guilty whenever they experience anger, even if the situation justifies anger. Similarly, some clients experience fear or guilt in response to joy. One client responded with shame anytime she experienced fear because her family had taught her that fear was a sign of inherent weakness. Another client became angry anytime the therapist provided constructive feedback. An analysis of this response revealed warranted shame as a connecting link.

DBT uses exposure procedures to treat these maladaptive or secondary emotions in which an initial, warranted emotion serves as a stimulus and then a second, unjustified, emotion occurs as the response. For exposure to succeed, the therapist must clarify which emotions are warranted and unwarranted in the chain analysis. Critical to the success of exposure with secondary emotions, the therapist must remain clear about the cue, the affect elicited by the cue and the covert and overt behaviours elicited by the affect. The following case illustrates both of these points. At the beginning of treatment, a client reported experiencing fear in response to his own anger. He then drank or took drugs to decrease both emotions. His recent history of violence when angry and the fact that he had not yet learned any skills to control his anger, however, justified the fear response. The therapy thus initially focused on treating the anger, not the fear, to decrease the substance abuse. The client learned to manage his anger and stopped the violence and substance abuse. Unfortunately, he continued to respond with fear to even moderate levels of warranted anger. He acted on the fear and avoided the anger by avoiding situations with any existing or potential interpersonal conflict. If he began to feel anger toward the therapist during a session, he would leave the session prematurely even if the anger were warranted. At this point in treatment, the therapist decided to use exposure to treat the fear and leaving the session early. In this case, the cue was the anger, specifically the physical tensing of the muscles, a "sense" of anger and negative judgements of the therapist. The affect was fear. Besides leaving the session, maladaptive behaviours included "pushing away" the judgements, inhibiting appropriate expressions of frustration with the therapist and worrying that, "I'm going to get in trouble if I get angry". The therapist first conducted imaginary exposure with the client, using the last episode of leaving as the imaginary scene. Applying the principles of exposure, the therapist helped the client to focus his attention on experiencing the sensations associated with his anger in that scene and to maintain this attention, without escalating or avoiding the sensations, until the fear itself peaked and declined. The therapist also had the client practise allowing his judgements to come and go and appropriately expressing his frustration with the therapist. After this initial use of exposure, the therapist tried to use *in vivo* exposure whenever the client became frightened by his own anger during a session.

22

Managing contingencies in the therapeutic context

DBT applies contingency-management procedures when skilful behaviour has been either punished or not reinforced or maladaptive behaviour has been reinforced. DBT increases skilful behaviour by eliciting internally reinforcing skilful behaviours (e.g. emotion-regulation skills reduce emotional distress, mindfulness reduces paranoid ideation), by helping the client to elicit or arrange effective reinforcement in the natural environment (e.g. interpersonal skills lead to husband decreasing unwanted sexual demands, family agrees to allow an adolescent more freedom if he returns to school) and by directly applying reinforcing consequences within the therapy context (e.g. problem solving by a client who wants therapist involvement leads to a longer session with the therapist). DBT decreases problematic behaviour through extinction (e.g. the husband no longer bandages his wife's wounds when she has cut herself because she felt lonely) and the judicious utilization of punishment (e.g. continuing non-collaboration by a client who wants therapist involvement leads to a shorter session with the therapist).

DBT differs from traditional contingency management in the degree to which it attends to and uses therapist responses to shape client behaviour. In almost every relationship, individuals respond to each other in ways that, intentionally or unintentionally, change the probability of the other engaging in a given behaviour. Unfortunately, change can easily occur for the worse. Many clients, for example, have a history of receiving desired responses from therapists (e.g. extended session time, more sympathy or soothing, or decreased demands) as a consequence of suicidal communications. Such responses often decrease the behaviour in the short term, but inadvertently reinforce it in the long term. DBT individual therapists must be acutely aware of how their responses influence clients and use this influence strategically to help clients. In contrast to the last example, many clients have had the experience that stopping suicidal behaviour or decreasing hospitalization has caused therapists to reduce availability, against the clients' wishes. Aware of this potentially punishing contingency, a DBT therapist generally reverses the contingency and agrees to renew a therapy contract only if the client has decreased target behaviours and increased skills use during the current contract period.

In-session behaviours often provide the best opportunities to use therapist responses to shape client behaviour. DBT utilizes contingency management to respond to relevant in-session behaviours, applying the procedures to reinforce skilful, collaborative behaviours and to extinguish or punish maladaptive, therapy-interfering behaviours. Common reinforcing therapist responses for adaptive client behaviours (e.g. collaborating, independently noticing judgements, spontaneously generating solutions or fully participating in skills rehearsal) include increasing validation, expressing more concern or interest, decreasing attempts to control the client and offering to extend or shorten the session according to the client's wishes. Maladaptive behaviours, however, usually require the withdrawal of reinforcement. For example, clients who want to avoid analysing a specific behaviour often will repeat automatically, "I don't know", or, "I can't remember", in response to therapists' questions because they have learned in other contexts that such responses may block additional questions and stop the analysis. In such cases, DBT therapists may successfully extinguish the behaviour by persisting with the questions or otherwise continuing the analysis until the problematic behaviour has stopped. Less frequently, therapists may use punishment. For example, if a client finds the therapist's approval or attention desirable, the therapist might withdraw the approval or attention in response to therapy-interfering behaviour. When the client ceased the behaviour and engaged collaboratively with the therapist, the therapist would respond again with approval or attention. Such a change in response by one individual to another's behaviour more closely resembles the contingencies in relationships outside of therapy than would constant approval or attention. In another example, whenever the therapist rehearsed mindfulness with the client, the client would mindfully describe one thought and then immediately (and perhaps wilfully) deliver a set of unmindful thoughts. Motivational rather than skills deficits maintained the problematic behaviour. Highlighting and gaining insight into the pattern did not change it, nor did extinction have any obvious impact. Then the therapist began to assign additional mindfulness homework whenever the behaviour occurred. After receiving only two or three additional assignments within the session, the client became motivated to remain mindful as long as possible.

Regardless of the specific behaviour or context, several principles remain important when using contingency management to decrease any problematic behaviour. Critical to using contingencies strategically, the therapist first should assess the reinforcing consequences or function of the target behaviour and base the application of contingency procedures on this understanding. The therapist can then identify opportunities to extinguish the behaviour by working with the client to remove reinforcing consequences. When considering extinction, of course, the therapist must attend to whether the client, the treatment team and the wider system can tolerate a behavioural burst without reinforcing an escalation of the behaviour. Equally essential, the therapist and client should identify alternative adaptive behaviours and their reinforcing consequences and shape these behaviours. With an understanding of the function of the problematic behaviour, they can particularly focus on more skilful ways to achieve the client's objectives.

The following case illustrates the principles highlighted above. A therapist applied contingency management as part of the intervention to reduce a suicidal client's refusal to dispose of a lethal stockpile of medications that he regularly took when overdosing. The client also sometimes increased his suicidal communications when the therapist persisted with requesting the disposal. A brief analysis of these behaviours revealed that the refusal functioned not only as an attempt to block the therapist's requests but also as a way to reduce the anxiety that he felt when he contemplated not having the stockpile. Though the therapist did not want to spend an entire session targeting the refusal or to insist that the client destroy the medication immediately, she equally did not want to reinforce the problematic behaviours. She attempted to minimize the reinforcement and extinguish the behaviours by continuing to target them at least until the client committed to working on disposing of the medication over time and the suicidal communications ceased. As soon as the client made the commitment, the therapist reinforced this new behaviour by ending the discussion of disposal and returning to the focus of the session. Equally critical to solving the problem, the therapist helped the client to develop more effective solutions to manage his anxiety about not having the stockpile. The therapist reinforced the client's application of these solutions, particularly by validating the difficulty of the task. The more powerful reinforcement, however, was the reduction in anxiety that the client experienced when he implemented the solutions. Because of the severe danger of maintaining the stockpile, the therapist also responded with aversive contingencies. First, the therapist became less validating and easy going and more formal or business like in response to the refusal and suicidal communications. Second, the therapist began to "nag" the client briefly every week by highlighting that the stockpile remained a problem and asking when the client would dispose of it. Within a month or so, the client gave the remaining medication to the therapist. To reinforce the compliance, the therapist immediately stopped nagging.

23

Changing cognitive behaviours

Although DBT therapists employ many traditional cognitive restructuring procedures, the core principles of the treatment lead therapists to utilize a different range of interventions to change a client's thinking. DBT includes traditional cognitive restructuring strategies such as identifying automatic assumptions, looking for evidence, challenging core beliefs and generating alternative interpretations. When trying to shape more effective thinking, however, the therapy also considers interventions such as contingency management and mindfulness. In applying the range of interventions, therapists attend to cognitive processes, as well as cognitive content.

Based on behavioural theory, DBT conceptualizes the act of thinking as behaviour and postulates that such cognitive behaviour develops according to the principles of learning theory. As a result of a behavioural approach, therapists attend to both the antecedents and the consequences that control a specific cognitive behaviour. For example, strong emotion is as likely to cause cognitive distortions as cognitive distortions are to cause strong emotions. Therapists may generate solutions for these antecedents and consequences, as well as for the cognitive behaviour itself. Thus, contingency management can increase or decrease the frequency of cognitive behaviours just as it does overt behaviours. For example, thinking "I can't" may have originally developed as a result of the invalidating comments of others or multiple failure experiences. At some point, however, the behaviour may have begun to function as a way to gain permission to avoid difficult tasks or situations. If a therapist identifies such a relationship, he or she might reduce the "I can't" thinking by including extinction in the solution analysis.

Consistent with Zen practice, DBT shapes cognitive behaviours through acceptance strategies and mindfulness. Linehan (1993a) contrasted DBT with traditional CBTs by highlighting the greater emphasis in DBT on validating cognitive behaviours whenever possible. The therapy also uses mindfulness as an alternative to cognitive restructuring. When treating judgemental thinking, for example, DBT therapists encourage mindfulness to reduce judging altogether rather than solutions that replace negative judgements with positive ones. Mindfulness emphasizes developing effective thinking over "right" or rational thinking. The following vignette illustrates these key points. An out-patient DBT client living in a residential unit expressed her belief that staff at the unit hated her and wanted, "To get rid of me". When she ruminated on these beliefs, she experienced shame and self-harm urges. Despite sounding extreme, the therapist knew from conversations with the staff that the client's thoughts closely paralleled the facts. The client's threatening and otherwise disruptive behaviours on the unit had led to most staff wanting to discharge her and to a few staff feeling extremely angry toward the client. The therapist wanted to decrease the ruminating because of the link to self-harm, but did not want to invalidate the valid and thus excluded such traditional techniques as looking for evidence. The therapist began by accepting the valid aspects of the client's thoughts but then highlighted the ineffective consequences of ruminating, even on valid beliefs. With coaching, the client then learned to describe the thoughts and their consequences more mindfully and to refocus attention on more effective ways of thinking such as how to both decrease threatening behaviour and improve her relationship with staff. If the therapist had not known the facts about the staff, she could have suggested a more dialectical solution analysis that included assessing the effectiveness of both mindfulness and cognitive restructuring.

24

Being dialectical

The dialectical strategies permeate the application of all other DBT strategies. They refer both to the continual re-balancing between acceptance and change in the use of other strategies and to a specific set of techniques that inherently include elements of acceptance and change. To progress dialectically, the therapist must attend to the entire context of a problem and learn how the various elements influence each other. The therapist must also embrace the conflicts that arise as opportunities to develop further. Though being dialectical may prove the most effective way forward, it is seldom easy. Success requires comprehensive assessments, rapid movement among the strategies and rigorous application of the treatment as a whole. Furthermore, the therapist must balance adherence to the treatment manual with responsiveness to the client, just as a ballroom dancer must follow both the steps of the dance and the movements of his or her partner. Indeed, therapy may seem rather like dancing with a partner, albeit sometimes dancing by the side of a cliff on rocky ground in a fog.

The therapist acts dialectically, in part, by interweaving change strategies with acceptance strategies. Most often this involves balancing problem solving with validation. Indeed, one could think of the relationship between these strategies as being like a healthy sandwich, with the problem-solving strategies as the meat and the validation strategies as the bread that holds it all together and prevents it from becoming a mess. The stylistic and case-management strategies described below, however, also require balance. For example, one client had several court cases pending for minor offences when he started DBT. On the acceptance side, the client's individual therapist knew that if she intervened in the environment by testifying in court about the client's treatment, she would increase the chances of the client receiving probation and the possibility of continuing treatment. The therapist balanced this acceptance of the client's current situation and capacities with strategies to change those capacities. She taught the client the distress-tolerance and emotion-regulation skills necessary to prevent the client from making the situation worse (he had urges to flee the jurisdiction) and to cope during his appearance in court. Furthermore, she made her willingness to recommend that the court allow him to continue treatment contingent upon him actually using these skills.

Specific dialectical techniques all share an inherent synthesis of acceptance and change that promotes movement. When using the technique of "making lemonade out of lemons", for example, the therapist validates the sourness of the client's situation and helps the client discover ways to sweeten the situation. While telling stories or sharing metaphors, the therapist tries both to communicate an acceptance of the client's position and to present an alternative that will help the client to progress. For example, one suicidal client wanted treatment to begin by processing her childhood trauma (Stage 2 work), despite the fact that such interventions had previously made her more suicidal. Comparing the processing of the trauma with reaching a mountain summit, the therapist validated the client's ultimate goal. The therapist also stated, however, that she would no more begin this work until the client had the requisite abilities than she would start climbing a mountain without the proper knowledge and equipment because people have died that way. The metaphor helped the client accept a synthesis between the two positions, namely that the work of Stage 1 was the preparation for a safer journey through Stage 2. A therapist may also elicit movement through the art of persuasion in the manner of ancient Greek philosophers who employed dialectics as a method of debate that involved refuting an opponent's argument by hypothetically accepting it and then leading the opponent to admit that it implies contradictory conclusions. In one case, a behavioural analysis with a client in a secure setting revealed that the patient cut herself in part because it gave her a sense of being in control. The therapist vigorously validated the client's goal to gain control and then proceeded to highlight how the staff perceived the cutting as a sign that the client had little self-control and needed more staff intervention to control her. This strategy alone did not change the client's cutting, but it substantially shifted her motivation to change it.

Other dialectical strategies include allowing natural change, playing devil's advocate, activating wise mind, conducting a dialectical assessment, entering the paradox and extending. We discussed allowing natural change and playing devil's advocate in Points 3 and 15 on the dialectical philosophy and pre-treatment, respectively. To activate wise mind, the therapist encourages the client to integrate her emotional experience with her logical thoughts. Conducting a dialectical assessment refers to considering the impact of all systems (e.g. biological, cultural and financial, as well as psychological) relevant to the client and often asking whether anything has been forgotten or ignored.

Entering the paradox requires therapists to highlight contradictions as they arise and to help clients tolerate them until they can resolve the paradox by finding a synthesis of the various positions. For example, one client frequently responded to the needs of others at the cost of caring for herself, because she valued them more. The therapist highlighted that caring for oneself is caring for others. In the case of a client with a history of hospitalizations that reinforced suicidal behaviour, the therapist told the client that she was too suicidal for hospitalization. For a client whose parents punished him for weakness whenever he cried, the therapist presented the paradox that crying is a sign of strength. The presentation of paradoxes in DBT resembles the *koans*, or practices, presented to students in Zen (Suler, 1989). In both, the solution arises through experiencing rather that analysing. The ultimate paradox in Zen, for Westerners at least, may be the coupling of the proposition that "the essential world of perfection is this very world" (Aitken,

1982, p. 63) with the proposition that "life is suffering" (Aitken, 1982, p. 49).

Extending is a translation of a technique employed in Aikido, a Japanese martial art (Saposnek, 1980; Windle & Samko, 1992). In extending, the therapist alters the direction of the session by unexpectedly accepting and extending an attack by the client. Doing so disarms or unbalances the client and enables the therapist to change course without harm to either person. The therapist joins with the client, allows the behaviour to progress naturally to the point intended by the client and then extends the behaviour beyond the point intended by the client. For example, a client may say, "You're a horrible therapist, I'm going to write a complaint about you", with little intent of writing a complaint but with the expectation that the therapist will resist the client's threat and will focus on repairing any damage to the therapy relationship to prevent the client from writing. A therapist using extending, however, would accept the client's desire to write such a letter and, extending the client's threat, may offer to spend the session time helping the client to write the letter because it is the therapist's job to help the client to be as effective as possible in writing the letter.

25

Using self-disclosure

Self-disclosure forms part of the reciprocal communication strategies, one of the two sets of stylistic strategies in DBT. The two styles of communication, reciprocal and irreverent, dialectically oppose each other, with reciprocal communication forming the acceptance pole. Key aspects of this style, such as warmth and genuineness, are common to many forms of psychotherapy. Reciprocal communication strategies, however, also include self-disclosure, a somewhat contentious area in psychotherapy. DBT identifies self-disclosure as a strategy that reflects one aspect of the radically genuine nature of the therapeutic relationship. Within the context of the professional role, the therapist expresses a willingness to reveal more information about him- or herself within the therapeutic relationship to enable clients to use the relationship as a mechanism to learn about themselves and about relationships more generally. For many clients, self-disclosure by the therapist also may motivate them to change.

In disclosing information to clients, therapists follow two general guidelines to ensure that the therapeutic relationship resembles as closely as possible aspects of non-therapy relationships and, crucially, remains within usual professional limits. First, therapists observe their own limits in relation to the frequency and content of self-disclosures; thus, some therapists disclose earlier or more often or reveal more personal information than others. Second, in addition to observing their self-disclosure limits, therapists remain vigilant to the impact of disclosure on the client and titrate the amount of self-disclosure to ensure maximum effectiveness. DBT therapists must disclose only information in the best long-term interests of the client.

Distinctive types of self-disclosure

Modelling self-disclosures are characteristic of the coping model used in DBT. In a modelling self-disclosure the therapist shares with the client his or her experience of a difficulty and how he or she solved the problem using either the principles of the treatment or skills taught in the treatment. In using modelling self-disclosure, therapists only disclose past or resolved problems that provide an illustrative example for the client. Of course, the therapist should not use modelling self-disclosure as an opportunity to receive help from the client. Finally, DBT recommends modelling a coping rather than mastery model of skill use. Many clients may experience a mastery model as demotivating, believing that such a level of competence is beyond them.

The following clinical vignette illustrates the use of modelling self-disclosure. An adolescent client was preparing for her first day at a new job in a shop. The client engaged fully in rehearsing new skills relevant to her first day but expressed doubt about her capacity to use the skills because of the gulf between practising in session and executing the new skills *in situ*. The therapist validated the contrast in the degree of difficulty between therapy and the new job by sharing her own experience of overcoming flight phobia. The therapist first described how she had prepared and practised a number of skills in preparation for a particularly long flight. When the therapist said, "And the thing with flight phobia is that when the plane's up it's up—it can't be half-up and half-down!", the client understood that the therapist genuinely grasped her sense of the enormity of the task. The therapist then described utilizing mindfulness and anxiety-management techniques to cope with surges of anxiety during the flight. The therapist highlighted that only after a number of flights and frequent practise had she become a relaxed flyer. At each stage, the therapist rehearsed with the client how she might use the same strategies on her first day at work.

In *self-involving self-disclosure*, the therapist identifies his or her own responses to the client and communicates them directly to the client. For example, after a number of months working to improve her relationship with her alcoholic father, a client reported that her father had said that because she had given up alcohol he did not want to see her any more as she reminded him of his own failures. As she described these events, the client was evidently sad. The therapist said, "I too feel sad about his decision, especially after how hard you've worked both to stop your alcohol abuse and to maintain your relationship with him". The client looked up following this remark and became more active in considering how she might manage not seeing her father.

Functions of self-disclosure

As with all strategies in DBT, therapists use self-disclosure strategically. For example, a therapist self-disclosure about managing a problematic emotion may motivate a client embarrassed about her own emotional responses to share relevant information with the therapist. Self-involving self-disclosure by the therapist may provides an opportunity for the client to learn about the interpersonal consequences of his or her behaviour and possibly motivate the client to modify behaviours that damage relationships. For example, a client frequently aggressively threatened suicide and blamed the therapist for his ineptitude in treating her. After a number of such incidents, the therapist said to the client, "When you threaten to kill yourself and blame me for not helping you, my motivation to help you decreases". In this example, the therapist discloses the impact of the client's behaviour on him to draw the interpersonal impact of the client's behaviour to her attention and to highlight possibly undesirable consequences of her behaviour. Assuming that the client wants the therapist to remain motivated to help, this self-involving self-disclosure may punish suicidal threats and motivate the client to modify her behaviour. In this case, the client was motivated to solve the problem and stopped threatening suicide. The therapist then coached the client in how to communicate her distress and frustration more effectively.

26

Confronting and being irreverent

Irreverent strategies provide the dialectical contrast to the reciprocal communication strategies of warmth, genuineness and self-disclosure. The therapist employs irreverent strategies when the client or client and therapist become stuck in a dysfunctional pattern of emotions, thoughts or behaviours. Metaphorically, therapists use irreverence when the therapy train appears in imminent danger of crashing at high speed into the buffers, and only diverting the train will avert an accident; irreverence is the verbal equivalent of changing the points. Although irreverence differs substantially from the reciprocal strategies, it also must arise from genuine compassion towards the client, not from a position of frustration and anger. Irreverence aims to help the client alter his or her perspective and let go of rigidly held views. Employing irreverence in anger reduces the likelihood of a shift in perspective by the client and increases the possibility that the client will hold more firmly to the very perspective that the therapist hopes to change.

DBT as a therapeutic approach recognizes the heightened sensitivity and vulnerability of individuals with a BPD diagnosis; however, the treatment also acknowledges that individuals with the diagnosis have a degree of robustness that is often underestimated. Irreverence addresses these non-fragile aspects of the client. Linehan (1993a) described several different types of irreverence. Some of these strategies are based primarily on tone. Most commonly, the therapist uses a matter-of-fact tone with the client when most therapists would become more validating or warm. For example, when a client reports a wish to die, professionals and non-professionals alike tend to respond with increased warmth, concern and interest. For many clients with a

BPD diagnosis, over time this response has reinforced suicidal communication as a way of expressing distress. The DBT therapist's absence of an increase in warmth and maintenance of a matter-of-fact tone in response to such communications represents the most basic level of irreverence. The unexpected nature of the response may grab the client's attention and assist the client to consider more effective ways of communicating distress. By using a matter-of-fact tone, the therapist begins to extinguish suicidal communication by removing a historical reinforcer of the behaviour. Thus, as with many strategies within the treatment, irreverence can function to manage contingencies within the therapeutic relationship. The therapist may move beyond a matter-of-fact tone and increase the intensity of the irreverent response by becoming more directly confrontational. For example, a client called her therapist following a last-minute cancellation by a friend of a meeting for coffee. The client threatened suicide saying, "Everything is hopeless—everyone always leaves me", and began to rehearse past endings of relationships. The therapist quickly blocked this behaviour with, "Stop catastrophizing and focus on solving the problem".

Beyond irreverent strategies based more on tone, DBT encourages the use of irreverent strategies that rely even more on the content of the statement in addition to the tone. Two of these strategies are *plunging in where angels fear to tread* and *reframing the client's communication in an unorthodox manner*. In using the strategy of "plunging in where angels fear to tread" the therapist simply says directly and clearly what many would consider unsayable, without "beating about the bush" or "hedging bets". For example, a therapist conducting a chain analysis with a client who had self-harmed by mutilating her genitals asked matter-of-factly whether the client had found the act sexually arousing.

In *reframing the client's communication in an unorthodox manner* the therapist responds to the client's communication in an "off-beat" completely surprising way. For example, a young female client with a history of sexual abuse complained bitterly each week in individual therapy about male members of her skills group looking at her during the session. She also reported increasing frustration with young men looking at her outside of the therapy context. The client was a striking young woman who dressed in a way that was likely to attract attention. The therapist discussed a number of strategies to address the problem (e.g. the client changing her style of dress, radical acceptance that men tended to look at her, restructuring of her judgements about the observation that she attracted the attention of others), all to no avail. The young woman continued to complain yet remained unwilling to either tolerate the difficulty or implement strategies to solve the problem. Then one week when the client began her usual complaint and combined it with a threat to drop out of skills group, the therapist said, "I know, it's impossible—the only solution for you is to live in a convent—maybe that's what we should work on this week— how to get you into a closed order!" The young woman immediately saw the point and became more willing to implement the previously suggested strategies.

On occasion, an irreverent strategy can widely miss the mark and, instead of assisting the client to change, exacerbate his or her difficulty or distress. In such circumstances, the therapist moves rapidly to change strategy and if appropriate apologize and repair the relationship. Interactions of this type provide an opportunity for the therapist to model how to recover from an interpersonal rupture without being overly defensive, apologetic or overwhelmed by affect.

When the client shifts from an entrenched position to a more flexible consideration of his or her circumstances and options, the therapist switches rapidly back to the reciprocal strategies. In part, this switch reinforces the client's movement. Therapist movement between both poles of the stylistic dialectic also enables clients to tolerate the inherent challenge in the irreverent strategies. The constant movement between the two poles provides some of the momentum within the therapy and is a distinctive characteristic of the treatment in its own right.

27

Consulting to the client

Consultation to the client represents the change end of the dialectical approach to case management within DBT. In itself, a defined approach to case management is a distinctive characteristic of the treatment. Most CBT approaches, indeed most psychotherapies, do not provide principles to assist the therapist to manage interactions among the various therapeutic interventions clients receive or among the treatment providers delivering these different interventions. The absence of case-management guidance may occur simply because most psychotherapies were developed for uncomplicated Axis I disorders, which require fewer interactions and involve less conflict between treatment providers. For clients who have a diagnosis of BPD combined with multiple other diagnoses or social problems, receiving multiple interventions from multiple treatment providers occurs frequently. Also, given the frequent tendency for these clients both to request and to require help from their therapist in negotiating these myriad interventions and treatment providers, a treatment for this population requires some principles to guide therapists in managing their cases.

DBT aligns the case-management strategies with *consultation to the client* providing change and *environmental intervention* representing acceptance. The central guiding principle is straightforward: the DBT therapist intervenes in the environment on behalf of the patient if, and only if, the short-term gain of an intervention by the therapist is worth the long-term loss in learning for the client. In all other circumstances the therapist coaches the client on how to intervene in the environment to solve the problem him- or herself. Many other forms of psychotherapy describe similar principles to help clients manage interpersonal problems with family, friends and work colleagues. DBT, however, uniquely applies this principle to assist clients in negotiating care and resolving problems with other healthcare professionals. For example, a client discussed with his DBT therapist dissatisfaction with his consultant psychiatrist and her prescribing practices. Rather than initiating a discussion with the consultant about appropriate medication for the client, the therapist worked with the client on expressing his concerns to his consultant and appropriately requesting changes in medication. The therapist also assisted the client to tolerate the dissatisfaction with his medication regime in the short term, while trying to change the consultant's behaviour in the long term. In another case, a client with a comorbid eating disorder required regular monitoring of her blood potassium levels. Rather than the therapist writing to the client's general practitioner to request the medical intervention, the DBT therapist had the client make the request herself. Consulting to the client about his or her treatment also aims to increase the client's capacity and motivation to act as an agent in obtaining appropriate health and social care for him- or herself. Pragmatically, therefore, consultation to the client potentially reduces the amount of time professionals need to divert to communicating with each other rather than working with the client.

In principle, many mental-health professionals would willingly endorse consulting to the client. In practice, however, mental-health services frequently operate according to different principles and practices that emphasize regular direct communication between mental-health professionals, especially around risk and treatment planning. Practically, then, the DBT stance of consultation to the client requires a significant change in practice for many DBT therapists and also for those clients who previously have not had the responsibility of communicating with other professionals about their treatment. To ensure effective implementation of the strategy and to decrease misunderstandings in the transition to this approach, comprehensive orientation of clients and the system to the principle forms a useful first step. Subsequent elaboration of the rationale for the approach and its practical consequences may prove necessary in any given interaction to provide clarity to the client and his or her network. In discussions with the client, the therapist monitors the balance between environmental intervention and consultation to the client and, especially as treatment progresses, pushes the client to be more active in negotiating and obtaining appropriate care.

The consultation-to-the-client principle guides the therapist in how to respond when another treatment provider requests information or consultation about a client or asks the DBT therapist to solve a problem with the client. With regard to requests for information from the client's treatment network, generally the DBT therapist may give information about the treatment programme but will not discuss the client or his or her treatment without the client present. Likewise, DBT therapists do not write letters or make phone calls to other professionals about the client without the input or presence of the client. The principle of consulting to the client also determines how and whether the DBT therapist provides advice to other therapists, both DBT and non-DBT, about how to interact with the client. For example, if a non-DBT case manager asks the DBT therapist about how to proceed with a mutual client. Rather than making suggestions about how the case manager should proceed, the DBT therapist would simply support the case manager responding according to the case manager's normal practice. Finally, just as the DBT therapist does not intervene to solve problems with other professionals on behalf of the client, the DBT therapist does not intervene with clients on behalf of other professionals. For example, a member of nursing staff complains to a DBT therapist on an inpatient programme that she is irritated with the client for breaking the smoking rules. The DBT therapist would target this behaviour only if there were no other higher targets and the complaints risked burning out the therapist or jeopardized the client's place on the unit.

Applying the consultation-to-the-client approach presents particular challenges for the therapist when he or she disagrees with the client's preferred course of action. In dealing with this situation, the DBT therapist explains the reasons for his or her disagreement with the client's decision; he or she may also encourage the client to review the pros and cons of the decision. If the client persists with the original decision, the DBT therapist assists the client to pursue his or her chosen course of action as skilfully as possible. For example, a client during a particularly stressful period experienced increased suicidal urges. In the past she had often been hospitalized under such circumstances, and, unfortunately, hospitalization had reinforced suicidal behaviour. After the last hospitalization, the client and therapist had agreed that together they would endeavour to avoid hospitalization as a solution to crises in the future. Now in an impending crisis, the client's resolve wavered. The DBT therapist reminded her of previous experiences and their agreement and then reviewed their previous pros and cons analysis. The client remained adamant that she wanted hospitalization. Therefore, the DBT therapist switched to problem solving with the client how the client could most effectively obtain hospitalization while minimizing the likely reinforcing effects of this course of action. Notably, the therapist did not intervene to obtain hospitalization for the patient.

28

Treating the client's therapy-interfering behaviour

As within any relationship, tensions will arise between the therapist and client. Point 3 describes examples of such tensions. As illustrated in that Point, DBT therapists attempt to resolve such conflicts by searching for syntheses, particularly those that validate both sides and move the treatment toward agreed-upon goals. When therapy tensions have not been successfully resolved they often result in therapy-interfering behaviours. For example, if a therapist simply confronted a client about abusing drugs but never offered alternative solutions that could achieve the client's goal of regulating affect, the client may begin to lie to the therapist about taking drugs.

Whether as the result of a specific conflict with the therapist or of more general psychological factors, clients with BPD frequently engage in therapy-interfering behaviour. The frequency of such behaviour may partly explain why clients with BPD have tended to have poorer outcomes in traditional treatments when compared to clients without personality disorders. Linehan (1993a), however, particularly attended to these behaviours when she developed DBT. Therapy-interfering behaviours include behaviours that directly interfere with the application of the treatment (e.g. not attending the session, arriving drunk at a skills training group, leaving sessions early, not completing diary cards) and behaviours that decrease the therapist's motivation to apply the treatment (e.g. pushing the therapist's limits, frequently complaining about the therapist to other clinicians, constantly criticizing the therapist). DBT does not consider therapy-interfering behaviours simply as obstacles to avoid or overcome so that therapy can proceed. Instead, it treats them as examples of the behaviours that occur in clients' lives outside of therapy and as the most immediate opportunities to change those behaviours. For example, an analysis of not completing the diary card may reveal that the client experiences intense shame when acknowledging behaviours on the card and thus avoids the card. If a similar pattern of shame and avoidance appeared in the analysis of parasuicide, then treating the shame leading to avoiding the diary card may also help to decrease parasuicide.

When therapy-interfering behaviours occur, the client's individual therapist applies the standard DBT strategies, with a particular emphasis on the problem-solving strategies. Generally, the therapist would begin to treat the behaviour by describing the behaviour, without judgement or inferring intent, to the client. For example, a therapist would say: "You just threatened to harm yourself if I don't extend the session", rather than, "You're trying to manipulate me", or: "I've noticed that you seldom complete your homework", rather than, "I think that you're sabotaging the therapy". The therapist may then try to increase the client's motivation to change the behaviour by highlighting the aversive consequences of the behaviour (including the impact on the therapist) and linking a change in the behaviour to the client's ultimate goals. For example, the therapist might say, "When you phone me inappropriately it makes me want to stop all phone contact. You have also said that many of your friends have withdrawn from you because you have pushed their limits. Maybe if we solve the problem in therapy, you can use the same skills to keep your friends". The therapist would then conduct a brief behavioural and solution analysis of the behaviour and immediately implement solutions to change the behaviour. In the case of unwarranted shame leading to the avoidance of the diary card, the therapist would primarily apply exposure with the support of mindfulness and perhaps other CBT solutions. Many clients respond with "I can't" when a therapist suggests practising a new skill. This single response, however, has many possible reasons, and as the reasons vary so will the solutions. Some clients genuinely cannot use a skill because they have not learned it well enough, in which case more skills coaching may solve the problem. Alternatively, other clients have some ability, but they also have some fear of being overwhelmed with embarrassment while practising the skills. In the face of unwarranted fear, exposure may prove effective. Other clients have the ability, but they also have a bias toward assuming poor outcomes (e.g. "I can't do anything. I always fail") or other negative cognitions that interfere with using skills (e.g. "I shouldn't ask for anything for myself"). In these cases, therapists might utilize mindfulness or cognitive restructuring or both. Finally, clients may have the skill but they want to stop the solution analysis altogether and believe that "I can't" will stop it. Therapists may then apply contingency management, ending the solution analysis only after the therapy-interfering behaviour has ended.

As with other target behaviours, the treatment of therapy-interfering behaviours often involves multiple CBT procedures in a single solution analysis. In one case, a client would try to change the topic whenever the therapist started to generate solutions for the client's bingeing. A brief behavioural analysis revealed that in response to the therapist's solution generation, the client would immediately think, "I should have thought of that. I'm so stupid". These thoughts elicited shame that led to the client self-invalidating by oversimplifying the difficulty of stopping the bingeing. She would then think, "I can't change", and begin to feel despair. At this point she would try to change the topic to avoid the shame and despair. Whenever the client expressed judgements during the behavioural analysis, the therapist had her mindfully notice them and then describe the relevant facts. Mindfulness also helped with the self-invalidating statements. To reinforce this practice of mindfulness, the therapist validated the actual difficulty of decreasing bingeing. The therapist prompted the client to use "wise mind" to determine if not having solved the bingeing problem herself warranted shame. To address the "I can't" statements, the therapist suggested a combination of mindfulness (particularly noticing and focusing on effectiveness) and cognitive restructuring (particularly generating alternative explanations for not having stopped bingeing). After completing the analyses of the therapy-interfering behaviour, the therapist applied exposure to treat the unwarranted shame by continuing to re-present the cue of solution generation for bingeing until the client's shame peaked and naturally subsided. During this procedure, the therapist blocked any attempts to change the topic. The client also learned to act opposite to the emotional urges by thoughtfully evaluating and trying the solutions for bingeing and even by asking the therapist to generate more solutions. Though the therapist utilized validation and praise to reinforce the client's collaboration and hard work, the actual decrease in shame most strongly reinforced her use of skills and other interventions. Also, when the client began to fully participate again in the solution analysis of the bingeing, her despair disappeared.

29

Treating the therapist

Just as therapists treat clients' therapy-interfering behaviours, so too must they treat their own behaviours that stop or reverse the progress of the treatment. Examples of such therapy-interfering behaviours include invalidating the valid, failing to target properly, not engaging the client in active problem solving, treating the client as overly fragile or reinforcing suicidal behaviour. These behaviours may result from some combination of the therapist's personal issues, clinical skills deficits, strong emotions or cognitive distortions during the session, or contingencies imposed by the system. Often, the prompt for the therapist's problematic behaviour is the client's therapy-interfering behaviour. One therapist who had a habit of lecturing clients analysed this pattern of behaviour and discovered that it tended to occur when a client had remained unresponsive for a prolonged time. The therapist identified the assumption that she had not explained things clearly enough as the intervening link. Once the therapist recognized this pattern, she mindfully let go of the assumption and focused instead on using DBT to treat the client's unresponsiveness. Just as the therapist shapes the client's behaviour, so the client shapes the therapist's behaviour. With some clients, in particular, the transaction between client and therapist may be such that the client punishes therapeutic behaviour and rewards iatrogenic behaviour. For example, one can easily imagine that if a client became verbally aggressive every time the therapist tried to address a presenting problem, the therapist may become less likely to target that problem.

A strong emphasis on therapists applying the treatment to themselves to reduce their own therapy-interfering behaviour characterizes the treatment. Therapists employ the full range of problem-solving strategies, including skills practice, exposure, contingency management and cognitive restructuring to change their own problematic behaviour and associated links. For example, if intense anger leads to overtly hostile behaviours, a therapist might act opposite to the emotional urges by identifying something about the client to validate. If interpretations of the client's behaviour partially caused the anger, challenging the interpretations may prove useful. If the anger results in desirable self-validation, the therapist might try to block that reinforcing consequence. Perhaps most critical is conducting therapy as mindfully as possible. Mindfulness requires the therapist to attend to this moment and being effective, to let go of distracting thoughts and urges and to refocus on solving the problem at hand. The mindful therapist is less likely to have therapy-interfering behaviour, more likely to notice when it does occur and more effective in changing the behaviour.

Changing therapy-interfering behaviour usually first requires an acknowledgement of the behaviour. Therapists often identify their own problematic behaviours during a session, and many clients will capably assist their therapists in this endeavour. Role-playing or listening to session tapes during consultation team meetings can help the team to detect behaviours that the therapist missed. Acknowledging the problem may lead directly to generating and implementing solutions, but some problems will require more thoughtful analysis by the therapist or assistance from the consultation team.

Though the consultation team generally functions to treat therapist-interfering behaviours and otherwise support the therapist, it can also become a context for consultation-interfering behaviours. Common behaviours include missing consultation-team meetings, not adhering to the treatment model and violating consultation-team agreements. The consultation team treats these behaviours just as an individual therapist treats therapy-interfering behaviours. For example, a therapist missed several consultation teams in a relatively short period of time.

When the team highlighted the problem and suggested analysing it, the therapist simply responded that she had an unusual number of demands at the moment. The team persisted in obtaining a detailed behavioural analysis to determine what specifically had caused the therapist to decide not to fulfil her commitment to the consultation team and to schedule conflicting meetings. The analysis revealed two important sets of variables. First, the therapist did have an unusually high number of demands at the moment because she unmindfully had agreed to a number of requests, fearing what others might think of her if she said no. The team helped the therapist to develop a "wise mind" response in these circumstances, rehearsed saying "No" to requests and planned how the therapist could cope with any negative response to the "No". Second, the therapist experienced little anxiety about skipping the consultation team, partly because she did not view her attendance as important. In response to these links, the team described the negative consequences of her absence on them and also highlighted possible aversive consequences for her clients if she did not receive the required amount of consultation.

Despite the notable problems caused by these consultation-team-interfering behaviours, therapists often hesitate to address these problems. As described in Point 12, having an identified observer can help. Even observers will hesitate, however, if they worry about how others will respond. If the facts do not warrant such worry, challenging the worry thoughts and approaching rather than avoiding the task usually proves an effective combination. As part of challenging the worry, therapists may want to consider whether they really think of their colleagues as more fragile or volatile than their clients or as less capable of receiving feedback. In approaching the task, therapists should use the same variety of strategies that they use with clients, starting with describing the problem behaviourally. Addressing consultation-interfering behaviours may also require the observer first to manage his or her own judgements, interpretations, other cognitions or emotions. If a member of the team does have a history of responding in a problematic way to critical feedback, then the team has the task of treating this consultation-team-interfering behaviour as well.

30

Evidence for efficacy and effectiveness

DBT places a strong emphasis on empirical data to establish both the efficacy of the treatment and its effectiveness in clinical practice. Although a focus on empirical data does not differentiate DBT from most other cognitive-behavioural treatments, it is a defining characteristic of the treatment. This Point summarizes briefly the current evidence for the efficacy of DBT and outlines principles for clinicians to consider in the evaluation of effectiveness in clinical practice.

Efficacy of DBT

Linehan developed DBT to treat adult women with a diagnosis of BPD and a recent history of parasuicidal behaviour. Five randomized-controlled trials (RCTs) support the efficacy of the treatment for this client group. The initial randomized trial compared one year of DBT to treatment-as-usual (TAU) in the community (Linehan, Armstrong, Suarez, Allman, & Heard, 1991; Linehan, Tutek, Heard, & Armstrong, 1994). After one year, recipients of DBT had significantly fewer parasuicidal acts, less medically severe parasuicides, fewer psychiatric in-patient days, lower anger, higher social and global functioning, and higher treatment-retention rates (DBT = 83% vs. TAU = 42%). Although all participants showed improvements in depression and suicidal ideation, the changes in the two groups on these variables were equivalent. At one-year follow-up, treatment gains were generally maintained, if less marked (Linehan, Heard, & Armstrong, 1995). Linehan recently replicated this study with a more rigorous control condition, comparing one year of DBT to treatment by non-behavioural experts in the community (TBE; Linehan et al., 2006b). In intention-to-treat analyses, DBT participants were significantly less likely to make a suicide attempt, less likely to require hospital admission for suicidal ideation, and had lower medical risk across all parasuicidal behaviours. Recipients of DBT were also significantly less likely to drop out of treatment, and had fewer psychiatric hospitalizations and psychiatric emergency department visits.

Other research groups conducted the three other RCTs examining the efficacy of DBT for women with a borderline diagnosis. Koons and colleagues (Koons, Robins, Tweed, Lynch, et al., 2001) examined the efficacy of DBT for women veterans with a BPD diagnosis, only 40% of whom had a history of recent parasuicide. After six months of treatment, DBT participants had significantly greater reductions in suicide ideation, depression, hopelessness and anger expression compared to a predominantly CBT control condition. Both conditions were equivalent with respect to parasuicidal acts, treatment retention, anger experienced and dissociation. Verheul, Van Den Bosch, Koeter, De Ridder, et al. (2003) examined the efficacy of DBT compared to TAU for adult women with a borderline diagnosis referred from either psychiatric or addiction services in Holland. Participants in DBT had greater reductions in self-mutilation and self-damaging impulsive behaviours (e.g. substance misuse, binge eating, gambling). Additional analyses revealed that the impact of DBT on self-mutilating behaviour was greatest in those participants with the highest baseline rates of self-mutilation. Again the DBT arm of the trial had better retention rates. Follow-up at six months after treatment ended demonstrated that DBT sustained its gains in terms of lower levels of parasuicidal and impulsive behaviour and in alcohol use. Differences between treatments in drug abuse were not sustained (Van den Bosch, Koeter, Stijnen, Verheul, & Van den Brink, 2005). Clarkin, Levy, Lenzenweger, and Kernberg (2007) compared outcomes in adults (men and women) with BPD among three treatments, namely DBT, transference-focused psychotherapy (TFP) and a dynamic supportive treatment. All treatments demonstrated significant improvements in depression, anxiety, global functioning and social adjustment across the first year of treatment. Both TFP and DBT resulted in significant reductions in suicidality. TFP and supportive treatment were each associated with improvement in aspects of impulsivity. TFP significantly predicted change in irritability, and verbal and direct assaults. All of these studies, with the exception of Clarkin et al., utilized recognized adherence measures to ensure that the treatment delivered in the trial was DBT, thus providing a genuine test of treatment efficacy.

In addition to these efficacy studies with the population for whom Linehan developed the treatment, there have been several studies examining efficacy in different client populations or for similar client populations in different settings. Linehan adapted DBT to treat women with BPD and substance dependence (Linehan & Dimeff, 1997), and has since examined the efficacy of this modified version of DBT (Linehan, Schmidt, Dimeff, Craft, et al., 1999). DBT participants had greater reductions in substance abuse compared to TAU at one year. Retention rates were also greater in DBT (DBT = 55%; TAU = 19%). Psychiatric in-patient days, anger, social functioning and global functioning did not differ between the two conditions. During the four-month follow-up period, however, DBT recipients had significantly greater reductions in substance abuse and greater gains in global and social adjustment. In a second trial, women diagnosed with BPD and opioid dependence were randomized to either DBT for substance dependence or a control condition, which consisted of Comprehensive Validation plus 12-Step programme (Linehan, Dimeff, Reynolds, Comtois, et al., 2002). This control condition comprised individual therapy utilizing the DBT acceptance strategies (e.g. validation, reciprocal communication and environmental intervention) and Narcotics Anonymous meetings. All participants received replacement medication with levomethadyl acetate hydrochloride (LAAM).

Both treatments effectively reduced opioid use. The Validation plus 12-Step control condition had excellent treatment retention rates (100%; DBT 64%). Clients in the DBT group were more likely, however, to maintain treatment gains. In addition to adult out-patients with a BPD diagnosis, RCT data is available to support the use of DBT in the treatment of adult women with a diagnosis of binge-eating disorder (Telch, Agras, & Linehan, 2001) and for older adults with comorbid depression and personality disorder (Lynch, Morse, Mendelson, & Robins, 2003; Lynch et al., 2007). Controlled trial data also supports the use of DBT for adult clients with a BPD diagnosis in an in-patient setting (Bohus et al., 2004). Evidence also exists to suggest that DBT may be a cost-effective treatment (Brazier et al., 2006; Heard, 2000).

Effectiveness of DBT

Knowing that DBT is an efficacious treatment is essential when deciding whether to implement it. Whether DBT proves an effective treatment option for any given organization or client, however, requires attention to outcome measurement in routine clinical practice. DBT treatment programmes collect data on client outcomes to assess effectiveness in treatment delivery and to provide information to the hosting healthcare organization. The focus of DBT on life-threatening and seriously destabilizing behaviours proves helpful in this regard. Just as therapists wish to ensure that the risk and severity of their clients' problems are decreasing, organizations want to reduce the frequency and severity of suicidal behaviours and to reduce the number of hospital days. Collecting data on these behavioural outcomes, therefore, benefits therapists and organizations alike. In addition to evaluating behaviourally specific outcomes targeted by the treatment (i.e. variables that the programme anticipates will change), DBT teams keep the evaluation task manageable and choose outcomes that link to stakeholder (client, family, therapist, and organization) goals (Rizvi, Monroe-DeVita, & Dimeff,

2007). Outcomes from these evaluations can only deliver a verdict on the effectiveness of DBT if measures of both programmatic and therapist adherence to DBT principles are taken.

In addition to the programmatic level, DBT therapists evaluate the impact of the treatment on individual clients' identified targets (Point 16). In most cases, outcome on these variables relates directly to the programme evaluation (e.g. parasuicidal acts, in-patient days) but will also likely include outcomes on idiographic variables (e.g. bingeing and vomiting episodes, frequency of stealing). Tracking outcomes for individual clients frequently proves helpful in treating clients with multiple comorbid conditions. At any one time, the size and number of tasks still to achieve in therapy may overwhelm therapists and clients alike, leading them to forget progress on previous targets. Outcome information can counteract this cognitive bias and provide more realistic assessments of treatment effectiveness. Such an objective evaluation of progress on target behaviours also assists the therapist and client to decide whether to continue therapy at the end of the treatment contract.

References

Aitken, R. (1982) *Taking the Path of Zen*. San Francisco: North Point.

American Psychiatric Association (2000) *Diagnostic and Statistical Manual of Mental Disorders (DSM-IV-TR)*, 4th edn. text revision. Washington, DC: American Psychiatric Association.

Arkowitz, H. (1989) "The role of theory in psychotherapy integration", *Journal of Integrative and Eclectic Psychotherapy*, 8: 8–16.

Arkowitz, H. (1992) "Integrative theories of therapy", in D. Freedheim (ed.), *The History of Psychotherapy: A Century of Change*. Washington, DC: American Psychological Association.

Barlow, D. H. (1988) *Anxiety and Its Disorders: The Nature and Treatment of Anxiety and Panic*. New York: Guilford Press.

Barwick, M. A., Boydell, K. M., Stasiulis, E., Ferguson, H. B., Blasé, K. and Fixsen, D. (2005) *Knowledge Transfer and Implementation of Evidence-Based Practices in Children's Mental Health*. Toronto, Canada: Children's Mental Health Ontario.

Basseches, M. (1984) *Dialectical Thinking and Adult Development*. Norwood, NJ: Ablex Publishing.

Bateman, A. W. and Fonagy, P. (2004) *Psychotherapy for Borderline Personality Disorder: Mentalization Based Treatment*. Oxford, UK: Oxford University Press.

Beck, A. T., Rush, A. J., Shaw, B. F. and Emery, G. (1979) *Cognitive Therapy of Depression*. New York: Guilford Press.

Bohus, M., Haaf, B., Simms, T., Limberger, M. F., Schmahl, C., Unckel, C. et al. (2004) "Effectiveness of inpatient dialectical behavioural therapy for borderline personality disorder: A controlled trial", *Behaviour Research & Therapy*, 423: 487–999.

Brazier, J., Tumur, I., Holmes, M., Ferriter, M., Parry, G., Dent-Brown, K. et al. (2006) *Psychological Therapies Including Dialectical Behaviour Therapy for Borderline Personality Disorder: A Systematic Review and Preliminary Economic Evaluation*. London: Queens Printer and Controller of HMSO.

Cialdini, R. B., Vincent, J. E., Lewis, S. K., Catalan, M., Wheeler, D. and Darby, B. L. (1975) "Reciprocal concessions procedure for inducing compliance: The door-in the-face technique", *Journal of Personality and Social Psychology*, 32: 206–215.

Clarkin, J. F., Levy, K. N., Lenzenweger, M. F. and Kernberg, O. F. (2007) "Evaluating three treatments for borderline personality disorder: A multiwave study", *American Journal of Psychiatry*, 164: 922–928.

Corsini, R. J. and Wedding, D. (1989) *Current Psychotherapies*, 4th edn. Itasca, IL: Peacock Publishing.

Fixsen, D. L., Naoom, S. F., Blasé, K. A., Friedman, R. M. and Wallace, F. (2005) *Implementation Research: A Synthesis of the Literature*. Tampa, FL: University of South Florida, Louis de la Parte Florida Mental Health Institute, The National Implementation Research Network.

Foa, E. B. and Rothbaum, B. O. (1998) *Treating the Trauma of Rape: Cognitive-Behavioral Therapy for PTSD*. New York: Guilford Press.

Frances, A. J., Fyer, M. R. and Clarkin, J. F. (1986) "Personality and suicide", *Annals of the New York Academy of Sciences*, 487: 281–293.

Freedman, J. L. and Fraser, S. C. (1966) "Compliance without pressure: The foot-in-the-door technique", *Journal of Personality and Social Psychology*, 4: 195–202.

Fruzzetti, A., Santisteban, D. A. and Hoffman, P. (2007) "Dialectical behavior therapy with families", in L. A. Dimeff and K. Koerner (eds), *Dialectical Behavior Therapy in Clinical Practise: Applications Across Disorders and Settings*. New York: Guilford Press.

Goldfried, M. R., Linehan, M. M. and Smith, J. L. (1978) "Reduction of test anxiety through cognitive restructuring", *Journal of Consulting and Clinical Psychology*, 46: 32–39.

Goldman, M. (1986) "Compliance employing a combined foot-in-the-door and door-in-the-face procedure", *Journal of Social Psychology*, 126: 111–116.

Gottman, J. M. and Katz, L. F. (1990) "Effects of marital discord on young children's peer interaction and health", *Developmental Psychology*, 25: 373–381.

Hall, S. M., Havassy, B. E. and Wasserman, D. A. (1990) "Commitment to abstinence and acute stress in relapse to alcohol, opiates and nicotine", *Journal of Consulting and Clinical Psychology*, 58: 175–181.

Hanh, T. N. (1987) *The Miracle of Mindfulness: A Manual of Meditation*, revised edn. Boston: Beacon Press.

Hayes, S. C., Follette, V. M. and Linehan, M. M. (2004) *Mindfulness and Acceptance: Expanding the Cognitive-Behavioral Tradition*. New York: Guilford Press.

Heard, H. L. (2000) "Cost-effectiveness of dialectical behaviour therapy for borderline personality disorder", *Dissertation Abstracts International Section B: Sciences & Engineering*, 61(6B): 3278.

Iwata, B. A. and Wordsell, A. S. (2005) "Implications of a functional analysis methodology for design of intervention programme", *Exceptionality*, 13(1): 25–34.

Jones, B., Heard, H. L., Startup, M., Swales, M., Williams, J. M. G. and Jones, R. S. P. (1999) "Autobiographical memory and dissociation in borderline personality disorder", *Psychological Medicine*, 29: 1397–1404.

Kabat-Zinn, J. (1991) *Full Catastrophe Living: Using the Wisdom of Your Body and Mind to Face Stress, Pain and Illness*. New York: Dell Publishing.

Kegan, R. (1982) *The Evolving Self: Problem and Process in Human Development*. Cambridge, MA: Harvard University Press.

Koons, C. R., Robins, C. J., Tweed, J. L., Lynch, T. R., Gonzalez, A. M., Morse, J. Q. et al. (2001) "Efficacy of dialectical behavior therapy in women veterans with borderline personality disorder", *Behavior Therapy*, 32: 371–390.

Kreitman, N. (1977) *Parasuicide*. Chichester, UK: Wiley.

Kremers, I. P., Spinhoven, Ph. and Van der Does, A. J. W. (2004) "Autobiographical memory in depressed and non-depressed patients with borderline personality disorder", *British Journal of Clinical Psychology*, 43(1): 17–29.

Kuhn, T. S. (1970) *The Structure of Scientific Revolutions*, 2nd edn. Chicago: University of Chicago Press.

Levins, R. and Lewontin, R. (1985) *The Dialectical Biologist*. Cambridge, MA: Harvard University Press.

Linehan, M. M. (1993a) *Cognitive-Behavioural Treatment of Borderline Personality Disorder*. New York: Guilford Press.

Linehan, M. M. (1993b) *Skills Training Manual for Treating Borderline Personality Disorder*. New York: Guilford Press.

Linehan, M. M. (1993c, January) *Acceptance in Dialectical Behaviour*

Therapy. Paper presented at the Nevada Conference on Acceptance and Change, Reno, Nevada.

Linehan, M. M. (1997) "Validation and psychotherapy", in A. Bohart and L. Greenberg (eds), *Empathy Reconsidered: New Directions in Psychotherapy*. Washington, DC: American Psychological Association.

Linehan, M. M. (1999) "Development, evaluation and dissemination of effective psychosocial treatments: Stages of disorder, levels of care and stages of treatment research", in M. G. Glantz and C. R. Hartel (eds), *Drug Abuse: Origins and Interventions*. Washington, DC: American Psychological Association.

Linehan, M. M., Armstrong, H. E., Suarez, A., Allman, D. and Heard, H. L. (1991) "Cognitive-behavioral treatment of chronically parasuicidal borderline patients", *Archives of General Psychiatry*, 48: 1060–1064.

Linehan, M. M., Comtois, K. A, Brown, M. Z., Heard, H. L. and Wagner, A. (2006a) "Suicide Attempt Self Injury Interview (SASII): Development, reliability and validity of a scale to assess suicide attempts and self-injury", *Psychological Assessment*, 18: 303–312.

Linehan, M. M., Comtois, K. A., Murray, A. M., Brown, M. Z., Gallop, R. J., Heard, H. H. et al. (2006b) "Two-year randomized controlled trial and follow-up of dialectical behavior therapy vs. therapy by experts for suicidal behaviors and borderline personality disorder", *Archives of General Psychiatry*, 63: 757–766.

Linehan, M. M. and Dimeff, L. (1997) *Dialectical Behaviour Therapy Manual of Treatment Interventions for Drug Abusers with Borderline Personality Disorder*. Seattle, WA: University of Washington.

Linehan, M. M., Dimeff, L. A., Reynolds, S. K., Comtois, K. A., Shaw-Welch, S., Heagerty, P. et al. (2002) "Dialectical behavior therapy versus comprehensive validation plus 12-step for the treatment of opioid dependent women meeting criteria for borderline personality disorder", *Drug and Alcohol Dependence*, 67: 13–26.

Linehan, M. M. and Heard, H. L. (1993) "Impact of treatment accessibility on clinical course of parasuicidal patients: In reply to R. E. Hoffman" [letter to the editor], *Archives of General Psychiatry*, 50: 157–158.

Linehan, M. M., Heard, H. L. and Armstrong, H. E. (1995) *Standard Dialectical Behaviour Therapy Compared to Individual Psychotherapy in the Community for Chronically Parasuicidal Borderline Patients*. Unpublished manuscript, University of Washington, Seattle.

Linehan, M. M. and Schmidt, H., III (1995) "The dialectics of effective treatment of borderline personality disorder", in W. O. O'Donohue and L. Krasner (eds), *Theories in Behaviour Therapy*. Washington, DC: American Psychological Association.

Linehan, M. M., Schmidt, H., Dimeff, L. A., Craft, J. C., Kanter, J. and Comtois, K. A. (1999) "Dialectical behavior therapy for patients with borderline personality disorder and drug-dependence", *The American Journal on Addictions*, 8(4): 279–292.

Linehan, M. M., Tutek, D. A., Heard, H. L. and Armstrong, H. E. (1994) "Interpersonal outcome of cognitive behavioral treatment for chronically suicidal borderline patients", *American Journal of Psychiatry*, 151(12): 1771–1776.

Lynch, T. R., Cheavens, J. S., Cukrowicz, K. C., Thorp, S. R., Bronner, L. and Beyer, J. (2007) "Treatment of older adults with co-morbid personality disorder and depression: A dialectical behavior therapy approach", *International Journal of Geriatric Psychiatry, Special Issue: Psychosocial Interventions for Mental Illness in Late-Life*, 22(2): 131–143.

Lynch, T. R., Morse, J. O., Mendelson, T. and Robins, C. J. (2003) "Dialectical behavior therapy for depressed older adults: A ran-domized pilot study", *American Journal of Geriatric Psychiatry*, 11(1): 33–45.

McMain, S., Sayrs, J. H. R., Dimeff, L. A. and Linehan, M. M. (2007) "Dialectical behavior therapy for individuals with borderline personality disorder and substance dependence", in L. A. Dimeff and K. Koerner (eds), *Dialectical Behavior Therapy in Clinical Practise: Applications Across Disorders and Settings*. New York: Guilford Press.

Miller, A. L., Rathus, J. H. and Linehan, M. M. (2007) *Dialectical Behavior Therapy with Suicidal Adolescents*. New York: Guilford Press.

Norcross, J. C. and Newman, C. F. (1992) "Psychotherapy integration: Setting the context", in J. C. Norcross and M. R. Goldfried (eds), *Psychotherapy Integration*, pp. 3–45. New York: Basic Books.

Pavlov, I. P. (1995) *Lectures on Conditioned Reflexes: Twenty-Five Years of Objective Study of the Higher Nervous Activity (Behaviour) of Animals*, W. Horsley Gantt, Trans. New York: Liverwright Publishing. (Original work published 1928)

Pryor, K. (2002) *Don't Shoot the Dog: The New Art of Teaching and Training*. Stroud, UK: Ringpress Books.

Reese, H. W. (1993) "Contextualism and dialectical materialism", in S. C. Hayes, L. J. Hayes, H. W. Reese and T. R. Sarbin (eds), *Varieties of Scientific Contextualism*, pp. 71–105. Reno, NV: Context Press.

Reps, P. and Senzaki, N. (1957) *Zen Flesh, Zen Bones*. Rutland, VT: Tuttle Publishing.

Rizvi, S. L. and Linehan, M. M. (2005) "The treatment of maladaptive shame in borderline personality disorder: A pilot study of 'Opposite Action'", *Cognitive and Behavioral Practice*, 12: 437–447.

Rizvi, S. L., Monroe-DeVita, M. and Dimeff, L. A. (2007) "Evaluating your dialectical behavior therapy program", in L. A. Dimeff and K. Koerner (eds), *Dialectical Behavior Therapy in Clinical Practise: Applications Across Disorders and Settings*. New York: Guilford Press.

Rogers, C. R. (1951) *Client-Centered Therapy*. London: Constable.

Saposnek, D. T. (1980) "Aikido: A model for brief strategic therapy", *Family Process*, 19: 227–238.

Shaw-Welch, S. (2005) "Patterns of emotion in response to para-suicidal imagery in borderline personality disorder", *Dissertation Abstracts International: Section B: The Sciences and Engineering*, 65(7-B): 3733.

Shea, M. T., Pilkonis, P. A., Beckham, E., Collins, J. F., Elkin, I., Sotsky, S. M. et al. (1990) "Personality disorder and treatment outcome in the NIMH treatment of depression collaborative research program", *American Journal of Psychiatry*, 147(6): 711–718.

Skinner, B. F. (1974) *About Behaviorism*. New York: Random House.

Steiger, H. and Stotland, S. (1996) "Prospective study of outcome in bulimics as a function of Axis II comorbidities: Long-term responses on eating and psychiatric symptoms", *International Journal of Eating Disorders*, 20: 149–161.

Stricker, G. and Gold, J. (eds) (1993) *Comprehensive Handbook of Psychotherapy Integration*. New York: Plenum Press.

Suler, J. R. (1989) "Paradox in psychological transformation: The Zen koan and psychotherapy", *Psychologia*, 32: 221–229.

Swales, M. A. (in preparation) *Implementing Dialectical Behaviour Therapy in Healthcare Systems: Utilizing the Principles of the Treatment to Effect Organizational Change*, in preparation.

Swann, W. B., Stein-Seroussi, A. and Giesler, R. B. (1992) "Why people self-verify", *Journal of Personality and Social Psychology*, 62: 392–401.

Tarrier, N. and Wykes, T. (2004) "Is there evidence that cognitive behaviour therapy is an effective treatment for schizophrenia? A cautious or cautionary tale?" *Behaviour Research and Therapy*, 42(12): 1377–1401.

Telch, C. F., Agras, W. S. and Linehan, M. M. (2001) "Dialectical behavior therapy for binge eating disorder", *Journal of Consulting and Clinical Psychology*, 69(6): 1061–1065.

Tucker, R. C. (ed.) (1978) *The Marx–Engels Reader*, 2nd edn. New York: W. W. Norton.

Van den Bosch, L. M. C., Koeter, M. W. J., Stijnen, T., Verheul, R. and Van den Brink, W. (2005) "Sustained efficacy of dialectical behaviour therapy for borderline personality disorder", *Behaviour Research & Therapy*, 43: 1231–1241.

Verheul, R., Van Den Bosch, L. M. C., Koeter, M. W. J., De Ridder, M. A. J., Stijnen, T. and Van den Brink, W. (2003) "Dialectical behaviour therapy for women with borderline personality disorder: 12-month, randomised clinical trial in The Netherlands", *British Journal of Psychiatry*, 182(2): 135–140.

Wang, T. H. and Katzev, R. D. (1990) "Group commitment and resource conservation: Two field experiments on promoting recycling", *Journal of Applied Psychology*, 20: 265–275.

Webster's New World Dictionary (1964) New York: The World Publishing Company.

Williams, J. M. G. and Pollock, L. R. (2000) "Psychology of suicidal behaviour", in K. Hawton and K. van Heeringen (eds), *The International Handbook of Suicide and Attempted Suicide*. Chichester, UK: Wiley.

Williams, J. M. G. and Swales, M. A. (2004) "The use of mindfulness-based approaches for suicidal patients", *Archives of Suicide Research*, 8: 315–329.

Windle, R. and Samko, M. (1992) "Hypnosis, Ericksonian hypnotherapy, and Aikido", *American Journal of Clinical Hypnosis*, 34: 261–270.

Yeaton, W. H. and Sechrest, L. (1981) "Critical dimensions in the choice and maintenance of successful treatments: Strength, integrity, and effectiveness", *Journal of Consulting & Clinical Psychology*, 49: 156–167.

Zanarini, M. C., Frankenburg, F. R., Hennen, J. and Silk, K. R. (2003) "The longitudinal course of borderline psychopathology: 6-year prospective follow-up of the phenomenology of borderline personality disorder", *American Journal of Psychiatry*, 160: 274–283.

Index